NUCLEAR DETERRENCE—THE DEFENSE SCIENCE BOARD'S PERSPECTIVE

HEARING

BEFORE THE

SUBCOMMITTEE ON STRATEGIC FORCES

OF THE

COMMITTEE ON ARMED SERVICES
HOUSE OF REPRESENTATIVES

ONE HUNDRED FIFTEENTH CONGRESS

FIRST SESSION

HEARING HELD
MARCH 9, 2017

U.S. GOVERNMENT PUBLISHING OFFICE

25–046   WASHINGTON : 2017

For sale by the Superintendent of Documents, U.S. Government Publishing Office
Internet: bookstore.gpo.gov   Phone: toll free (866) 512–1800; DC area (202) 512–1800
Fax: (202) 512–2104   Mail: Stop IDCC, Washington, DC 20402–0001

SUBCOMMITTEE ON STRATEGIC FORCES

MIKE ROGERS, Alabama, *Chairman*

TRENT FRANKS, Arizona, *Vice Chair*
DOUG LAMBORN, Colorado
DUNCAN HUNTER, California
MO BROOKS, Alabama
JIM BRIDENSTINE, Oklahoma
MICHAEL R. TURNER, Ohio
MIKE COFFMAN, Colorado
BRADLEY BYRNE, Alabama
SAM GRAVES, Missouri

JIM COOPER, Tennessee
SUSAN A. DAVIS, California
RICK LARSEN, Washington
JOHN GARAMENDI, California
BETO O'ROURKE, Texas
DONALD NORCROSS, New Jersey
COLLEEN HANABUSA, Hawaii
RO KHANNA, California

DREW WALTER, *Professional Staff Member*
LEONOR TOMERO, *Counsel*
MIKE GANCIO, *Clerk*

CONTENTS

Page

STATEMENTS PRESENTED BY MEMBERS OF CONGRESS

WITNESSES

APPENDIX

NUCLEAR DETERRENCE—THE DEFENSE SCIENCE BOARD'S PERSPECTIVE

House of Representatives,
Committee on Armed Services,
Subcommittee on Strategic Forces,
Washington, DC, Thursday, March 9, 2017.

The subcommittee met, pursuant to call, at 3:36 p.m., in room 2118, Rayburn House Office Building, Hon. Mike Rogers (chairman of the subcommittee) presiding.

OPENING STATEMENT OF HON. MIKE ROGERS, A REPRESENTATIVE FROM ALABAMA, CHAIRMAN, SUBCOMMITTEE ON STRATEGIC FORCES

Mr. Rogers. Good afternoon. The subcommittee will come to order. I want welcome to our hearing on "Nuclear Deterrence—The Defense Science Board's Perspective."

I want to thank all of our witnesses for being here today, and for your service to the public. Our witnesses are all experts who have spent their careers in fields related to nuclear deterrence. They are appearing today in their capacities as members of the Defense Science Board [DSB], but all have long and distinguished histories in the topic of our hearing today.

We thank you for the hard work it takes to prepare for this hearing.

And our witnesses are Dr. Michael Anastasio, Dr. Miriam John, and Dr. William LaPlante.

Without objection, I will introduce my full statement for the record, but I would briefly summarize.

In December 2016, in the waning days of the Obama administration, the Defense Science Board completed a report titled, "Seven Defense Priorities for the New Administration." It made recommendations to the new Trump administration on key issues in the world of defense. Chapter 2 of this report summarized years of work by the Board on nuclear deterrence, which is exactly what we will explore today.

The Board has published 12 studies over the 14 years on this topic. So it is clear the Board has spent a lot of time thinking about this, as well it should. A defense mission of this importance seems worthy of sustained and focused attention.

As the new administration and Congress goes forward with the nuclear modernization program initiated by President Obama, the Board's experts help us take stock. They help us understand how nuclear threats are evolving and how we should compensate. They help us understand where we have been and where we should go.

Our witnesses today will be able to provide the collective views and recommendations of the Board as well as their own views as Board members.

Ensuring a credible nuclear deterrent for the long-term future will continue to be a major priority for this Nation and the Congress and this committee.

With that, let me turn to my friend and colleague, the acting ranking member from Washington State today, Mr. Larsen, for any opening statement he may have.

[The prepared statement of Mr. Rogers can be found in the Appendix on page 23.]

STATEMENT OF HON. RICK LARSEN, A REPRESENTATIVE FROM WASHINGTON, SUBCOMMITTEE ON STRATEGIC FORCES

Mr. LARSEN. Thank you, Mr. Chairman.

Doctors, I join Chairman Rogers in welcoming you to the subcommittee. Thanks for helping us out.

Ranking Member Cooper is unable to participate in today's hearing. He is pretty ill right now, just sort of kind of a head cold and can barely speak. So I am sitting in for him, and I know he would be here if he could.

So as independent advisers, though, the DSB has an important role to play in making recommendations to the scientific and technical matters to the DOD [Department of Defense] leadership. And in its "Seven Defense Priorities for the New Administration" report, the DSB correctly noted that our nuclear forces remain a cornerstone of U.S. national security. I agree that this is one of the most important areas for the Department and for our community to focus on.

Given how critical these nuclear systems are and with costly modernization programs occurring concurrently, we can't afford to get this wrong. While I appreciate the vision represented in the report, I would be remiss if I did not mention that DOD still has been unable to provide us with a 30-year estimate on the full costs of nuclear modernization.

It is not a matter of partisan politics. Members of this committee have been asking for this accounting across multiple administrations.

In your report, you write that the budget for modernization, quote, "will significantly compromise investments in conventional capabilities," unquote. This commonsense observation should alarm those who seek to downplay the impact on the defense budget of nuclear modernization and provoke all of us to understand the inherent tradeoffs that are looming.

There are other elements of this report that I find concerning. You recommend prototyping and fielding low-yield nuclear weapons. I found the justification to be unclear. Are these intended to address new threats? To enable us to reduce our stockpile of other types of nuclear weapons? To deter a Russian escalate-to-deescalate scenario? Are they to keep nuclear weapon scientists sharp and interested in their mission?

These are all very different objectives. I have not seen a sufficiently detailed analysis of what the proposals are, whether they are necessary, what alternatives are being considered, what the tradeoffs are, what the costs would be, and, of course, what the policy implications are.

I also find this recommendation to run contrary to General Hyten's testimony yesterday. During the full committee hearing, General Hyten stated that the deployment of nuclear weapons is always an attempt to achieve strategic effects and disagreed with the distinction between tactical and strategic nuclear weapons.

Smaller nuclear weapons would require prototyping. However, Dr. Richard Garwin and Dr. Roy Schwitters, both of the eminent JASON scientific group, strongly criticized the need and value of manufacturing prototypes of new nuclear weapons in written comments to this subcommittee last year.

I am particularly concerned that new types of nuclear weapons would have significant policy and proliferation implications. Adding new military capability and building new nuclear weapons would be a radical shift, one that Congress, rightly so, has not been willing to approve for nearly 25 years. This approach could lead to a requirement for renewed nuclear testing, a policy shift that would be unwise, unnecessary, and have potentially disastrous consequences in re-legitimizing nuclear testing and helping to advance our adversaries' nuclear forces.

The DSB report more explicitly opens the door to the potential need to resume testing. Until now and for the foreseeable future, our top scientists have confirmed that there is no need to resume nuclear testing to certify the current stockpile.

Still, there is much to commend in your report. It highlights correctly, I believe—and we get ice cream sometimes with our Brussels sprouts—it highlights correctly, I believe, the need for investments in detection and monitoring technologies, which can reduce the threat posed by nuclear proliferation. With new technologies such as 3D printing emerging, these investments can support current and future nonproliferation and arms control agreements with a robust technological foundation.

The report also correctly identifies some of the geopolitical complexities that have challenged our nuclear deterrent. These include proliferation of nuclear weapons, and our allies' concerns that the U.S. may be weakening its security guarantees.

As a candidate, the President expressed support for proliferation and seemed to threaten the sanctity of the American security guarantee to our allies. It is my hope that as Commander in Chief, he understands the destabilizing effects of these statements.

A 2014 DSB report warned that, quote, "For the first time since the early decades of the nuclear era, the Nation needs to be equally concerned about both vertical proliferation, the increasing capabilities of existing nuclear states, and horizontal proliferation, an increase in the number of states and nonstate actors possessing or attempting to possess nuclear weapons. Monitoring for proliferation should be a top national security objective, but one for which the Nation is not yet organized or fully equipped to address," unquote.

Your comments and insights on this issue are most welcome. I would be interested in more specific recommendations in support of this mission, particularly with regard to what gaps remain and how we can use advancing technology and analytical approaches, including big data analytics, to improve our capabilities.

I want to thank you for joining us today. And I yield back, Mr. Chairman.

[The prepared statement of Mr. Larsen can be found in the Appendix on page 25.]

Mr. ROGERS. I thank the gentleman.

I want to let the witnesses know that their entire opening statements will be accepted for the record. If you would like to just spend your 5 minutes summarizing, that is fine—or less.

But I will take the first witness, Dr. Anastasio, for your opening statement—oh, okay. I understand that you have a joint opening statement?

Dr. ANASTASIO. Yes.

Mr. ROGERS. And Dr. John is going to present that to us.

And then the other two, if you have an opening statement you want to submit individually, we will take that for the record.

With that, you are recognized, Dr. John.

STATEMENT OF DR. MIRIAM JOHN, DR. MICHAEL ANASTASIO, AND DR. WILLIAM LAPLANTE, MEMBERS, DEFENSE SCIENCE BOARD

Dr. JOHN. Thank you. I lost the coin toss.

Chairman Rogers, Ranking Member Larsen, and members of the subcommittee, we thank you for the opportunity to testify today concerning "Nuclear Deterrence—The Defense Science Board's Perspective." And we are here representing the Defense Science Board.

We are going to discuss our principal findings and recommendations over the past 15 years' worth of work, and as you noted, they are summarized in chapter 2 of the report that we issued in December.

For those that are not fully familiar with the Defense Science Board, we are indeed a Federal advisory committee to the Secretary of Defense and a source of independent scientific and technical advice.

Our tasking, we do not invent our tasking. Our tasking comes from Department leadership and occasionally comes from you all, from Congress. And, typically, it is to address tough problems that may not have a lot of structure, like cyber and nuclear in the early days of its emergence, and/or problems it may present on the positive side, game-changing opportunities. We have done a lot of work in things like directed energy over time, autonomy, and electronic warfare.

There are currently 46 members of the Board, and we come from a wide variety of walks of life in the national security arena. The three of us represent, all right, over 100 years of experience in the nuclear area. And when we wrote that down, my God, I felt old.

All right. For the topic of this hearing, namely, the DSB's perspective on nuclear deterrence, we have summarized over a decade's worth of work in chapter 2 of our recently released "Seven Defense Priorities for the New Administration." Based on what you have already heard this week, and especially yesterday from our military leaders, you are probably not going to learn much new from us, because there is a lot of harmonization of views. It is just that we have been saying it a lot longer, I think, than they have.

Our working assumptions have always been that there is no more important defense objective than preventing a nuclear attack on the United States or its allies, and the foundation for prevention is deterrence.

Three key points that we would make around that, and you can find them in the report, although they are not stated quite this succinctly.

The first, the threat environment has been evolving in very troubling ways. Since the end of the Cold War, the United States has sought to raise the threshold for nuclear use, at least for ourselves, by emphasizing dramatically improved nonnuclear or conventional force capabilities.

Unfortunately, others have gone the wrong way—let's just say different directions—in part, because they can't afford to overmatch us conventionally. Russia has modernized and expanded the capabilities of its nuclear force. China has expanded both its nuclear and nonnuclear forces. And we face a new and unpredictable nuclear proliferator in North Korea.

We have also seen attempts at commerce in nuclear know-how and materials and acquisition—attempts at acquisition elsewhere, name them. North Korea, Libya, Pakistan, Iran are on the list.

The second point, modernization of the triad and the infrastructure to support it is long overdue. The triad remains a key component of the Nation's deterrence posture. The platforms and warheads have aged well beyond their original design intent. In addition, critical elements of the DOE [Department of Energy] production infrastructure are very old and inefficient. We simply can't wait any longer to renew all three legs of the triad and to assure their operational viability and readiness.

Our third point, and this is the one that may engender the most discussion, we must hedge against an uncertain future. We should expect—we already are, but we should expect that it won't change, that the future holds a very dynamic geopolitical environment for us, that the advances in science and technology are happening at a breathtaking pace and are happening on a global scale, and continued attempts by adversaries will be paramount in thwarting U.S. advantages.

To ensure a robust deterrence posture besides the triad, there is much more to the story, and we believe there also need to be healthy efforts to, one, deepen our insight into the developing capabilities, doctrine, and threats of current and potential adversaries. So we have got to keep an eye on what they are doing.

We need to ensure a very robust nuclear command and control and communication system. We need to ensure the survivability of U.S. forces, both nuclear and nonnuclear forces, in the face of their use of nuclear weapons. And we need to ensure a demonstrated, flexible, and adaptive capability to respond to changing threats through a strong research and development program.

And finally, and equally important, we need to prevent further proliferation through both cooperative and unilateral measures, through the tools of diplomacy, and through renewed and strengthened efforts at assurance of extended deterrence to our allies.

The linchpin of all this, of course, is the demonstrated skills of the talented, knowledgeable, committed, and valued people who are part of this enterprise.

With that brief background, we would be happy to take your questions.

[The joint prepared statement of Dr. John, Dr. Anastasio, and Dr. LaPlante can be found in the Appendix on page 28.]

Mr. ROGERS. I thank you. And I will recognize myself for the first set of questions.

The DSB report from December says that we should focus our nuclear weapons R&D [research and development] on concept and advanced development. Prototyping, placing options on the shelf should be needed rapidly. It goes on to say: Already, the DOD can anticipate the need for capabilities such as hardening or maneuvering for defensive penetration.

In this open forum and in more detail later, when we are in our classified session, would you please explain why the DSB and DOD anticipate needing to pursue capabilities like maneuverable warheads or lower yield, primary-only missile warheads?

Dr. ANASTASIO. Well, Mr. Chairman, I am trying to be careful.

Mr. ROGERS. Well, what you can't say here we will say in the classified.

Dr. ANASTASIO. No, I understand. I am just getting my thoughts right.

I think the issue is the developing capabilities in our adversaries like the Russians and the Chinese with more and more capable denial capabilities, denial our access for our systems. They have to believe that if we were ever—if a President ever made a decision to use it, that it would get to its target. And if they develop capabilities to try to deny us that, then we need to assure that we have alternate ways to do that.

And I think that is the origin of the thinking about how do you anticipate what might be coming from an adversary and have our deterrent be in a place where we can counter their capabilities. And so we should be thinking about the kinds of options that we in the military might have to do that. So how do you anticipate what a future threat might be and how are we going to be prepared to deal with that?

Mr. ROGERS. Based on the threats we see developing with our adversaries, when do you think we are going to need to be able to field these capabilities that you referenced?

Dr. ANASTASIO. Well, I think they are developing capabilities now, and we can talk more about that later. And I think it is it up to the military and the Defense Department and all the leadership of the country to decide what actually needs to get done when. But I think those capabilities are developing, and we can talk about that later.

Mr. ROGERS. Okay.

Dr. LaPLANTE. I would just add, Chairman Rogers, to my colleague that one of the things that the science and technology community must do is always understand the limits of what physics and engineering can be done. That is separate from what the threat is assessed to be.

So we have a duty to understand things like the maneuvering, what is capable technologically, and what could be done to counter it, both ways, offensive, defensive. We have to understand that and be ahead of a potential adversary.

So just from a technical edge and an engineering edge, we have to understand that, and then watch, as you say, as the threat evolves or if operationally there is a change, we can provide to the policy makers, to the leadership, what the technology can do or what it can't do.

Mr. ROGERS. Do warhead life extension programs truly utilize all the design, engineering, science, and manufacturing capabilities that would be needed to produce a new nuclear weapon?

Dr. ANASTASIO. Not completely, Mr. Chairman. What we are doing with the life extension programs is largely renewing the capabilities, the systems that we had during the Cold War. And in some cases, we are having to make some accommodation to the fact that certain materials and so forth are not available anymore. But, largely, we are replicating something that we had.

What we are not doing is exercising that full end-to-end partnership with the Department of Defense and DOE to think about what a requirement might be, how would you go implement that requirement with the constraints that get imposed, and then carry that all the way through to developing a weapon system out the door that could potentially go in the stockpile.

And we have not exercised that full system process since the end of the Cold War, for over 25 years. So there is a skill set that is involved in doing that process and that collaborative work between DOE and the DOD that we haven't fully exercised. Certainly, doing the LEPs [life extension programs] exercise is part of that, but not that full sweep.

Mr. ROGERS. What should Congress do to improve the stockpile responsiveness program to get after the problems you have described here in your report?

Dr. JOHN. We saw your authorization for the stockpile responsiveness program as a huge step forward, but it is authorized and it is not appropriated. So there needs to be some continued encouragement that DOE put money behind it, but it is also important that it is a partnership with DOD. And it is not on the radar screen at DOD to think about the future at this point, because there are trades to be made between what you put on the weapon, what you put on the delivery platform.

And across the board, they have got to be concerned about the new threats to new systems that we are putting forward. And I would throw out cyber as something that this community is just waking up to thinking about.

Mr. ROGERS. Okay. Thank you. The Chair recognizes the ranking member for any questions he has.

Mr. LARSEN. Thank you, Mr. Chairman.

So the 2014 report warned of this vertical proliferation and horizontal proliferation. It led to a provision in the NDAA [National Defense Authorization Act] at the time calling for a national roadmap, identifying costs, gaps, opportunities to partner with industry and academia that would improve nuclear verification. We are still waiting to get that report 3 years after the provision in the bill.

Do you think that report should be a priority for the administration to answer those questions?

Dr. JOHN. Well, since I was the prime mover behind that report, you would see me say, yea, verily. Because for one thing, technology has moved forward in ways that would allow us to do a much stronger job at what I would call early, early detection of proliferation where you have many more options to either cooperatively or unilaterally thwart the acquisition by a new proliferant.

I will say that my somewhat limited insight into things that have happened around a Presidential directive in the last administration created some working groups across the interagency. And I had the opportunity to spend the day with them about a year ago, and I have never seen so many different intelligence community representatives who knew each other and were sharing information.

Now, that is the good news. And you say, why is that happening? Well, it is a very small community still, so it has been easy to make the connections.

We on the Defense Science Board are about to publish another report that really hammers home this early, early warning piece and the potential for the tools of big data management and acquisition and data analytics and the promise that that holds, particularly when you tap into open source, for the sort of cueing that you would need on where to look and all. So continued emphasis on that, because it is a new paradigm for the intelligence community to step up to this.

Dr. ANASTASIO. Could I add one more thought to that? Which is that as technology evolves and as we do more R&D, you can imagine that the paths to proliferation can change. When we get in another room, we can talk more about opportunities like that that could be out there that would be nontraditional paths, and, hence, the R&D community needs to help the intelligence community understand what are the potential threats of the future that might come about and how would you look for those, too. So it is not just monitoring what you are used to monitoring, but, perhaps, there are other things you have to look for.

Mr. LARSEN. Would you argue, then, this could help us with detection and verification as well?

Dr. JOHN. We really didn't touch the verification problem in what we looked at. We started out to, because we had anticipated a more robust arms control agenda when we started the study in the 2010 timeframe, and that quickly fell apart. But at the same time, arguing among ourselves, we actually were taken with the fact that we have a problem with proliferation that seems to be cropping up in many different ways. And so let's take a step back and figure out if we have got the tool set to be able to deal with what we see coming.

Mr. LARSEN. Yes. Would you suggest that that be on our plate, the subcommittee, to look at that?

Dr. ANASTASIO. Verification?

Mr. LARSEN. Yes, the verification, the use of these new tools and how it applies to verification.

Dr. JOHN. I am not sure, because it depends on what treaties are going to be honored by our partners who have signed up and the like as to how much to put in a verification piece of it at this point.

Dr. ANASTASIO. I think there has been work done in the past to think about how you do verification on what potential agreements might look like, and if you get to the point where you are starting to count warheads themselves, the individual objects, how would you do verification of that and how could you agree on protocols for how to do that, et cetera. And there has been work done on things like that. And so that might be something that is worth the committee getting updates on. But it does depend on what you might think an agreement of the future might look like.

Mr. LARSEN. Yes. Okay. Thank you, Mr. Chairman. I will yield back to other members.

Mr. ROGERS. The Chair now recognizes the gentleman from Colorado, Mr. Lamborn, for 5 minutes.

Mr. LAMBORN. Thank you. And thank you for all the work that you have done on these important issues.

You talk about the lack of funding, and you talk about the modernization that Russia and China have done in recent years but we have not done because of lack of commitment and funding. And I think after meeting with some of the uniformed people that we have listened to this week, and previously also, we know the way forward. We just have to have the financial commitment to do the modernization and upgrading and enhancing reliability and safety and security.

If we don't do that, what is the risk that our nuclear umbrella has if it begins to develop leaks, if the 30 or so allies that rely on our nuclear umbrella have doubts as to whether we can actually carry through on our commitments? Will they begin to contemplate developing their own nuclear programs, for instance?

Dr. LaPLANTE. As you note, Congressman, the fact that we have put off modernization for lots of reasons until where we are today, where we basically have no more life extension that can be done, that is one of the reasons why we are in this situation today where you have in the 2020s all this stuff that has to happen at the same time. We can't push it anymore.

It is remarkable that we are flying the B–52s today in the nuclear mission. Grandfathers, sons, and grandsons, literally have the same airplane. It is absolutely remarkable. As a former chief of staff for the Air Force used to say, it would qualify for an antique license plate in the State of Virginia.

So I think, getting to your question about how does that deal with our allies, giving them confidence, well, no matter what you say in terms of your commitment, if you don't do it, and if you don't keep your systems current, people are watching. They are watching not just what you are saying, they are watching, are you really going to extend and go into the next version of *Ohio* replacement? Are you really going to build this bomber? Are you really going to do it and not just talk about it, not just study it? And we are sort of at that point where we are either going to do it or we are not, because, really, you can't life extend. So I would imagine everybody is watching what we do for all the reasons that you imply.

Dr. JOHN. Just to add a little color here, I guess. There are discussions that have been ongoing, I am sure you are all aware, in South Korea and Japan. They are not the majority yet, but the noise is there. And, my God, the last week, the Poles, the Germans said, maybe we better start thinking about a NATO European-owned deterrent. So we have got some fraying around the edges here. And so it is part what we do. It is also part what we back up with our words and actions.

Mr. LAMBORN. Let me ask about one other possible erosion of our nuclear umbrella, and that is the lack of testing. It has been 25 years since any tests have been done. I think we can be confident today that our weapons would still perform as needed, as advertised. But as each year goes by, we are going to lose, I believe, some of that certainty and the day will arrive when we need to negotiate with near peers about maybe a one-time round of testing and negotiate it.

What threat do we have—and I will disagree with my colleague to my left—what risk do we have if our credibility becomes eroded because people don't have confidence that the weapons will actually—or at least all of them will perform?

Dr. ANASTASIO. Let me try to take that one on, since I had the honor to write nine of the letters, annual assessment letters that go to the President and Congress about the need for testing. And I would reiterate that I believe and that I think the Defense Science Board believes that there is no need for testing right now. And the way I think about it is that nuclear testing is a tool. It is a technical tool to help us do a job. And our view is that the job we have today, we don't need that tool right now.

The question becomes, would I need it in the future? Well, the answer to the question depends on what my job is in the future. There are potential versions of the job, like the job we had in the Cold War, for which we would say we do need nuclear testing. But if the job looks like the one we have today, I think the view is that we don't believe that is an essential element, a tool, for us to get our job done with confidence. So it is a tool to be used, and it depends on what you are trying to accomplish when you do it.

The other piece is, as our chairman of the Defense Science Board reminds us, we should be humble about the future. We don't know what the future is going to look like in 10 or 20 years. And so to make a blanket statement about what it is we need or don't need then is probably a fool's game.

Mr. LAMBORN. Thank you.

Mr. ROGERS. Thank you. The Chair will now recognize the gentleman from California, Mr. Garamendi, for 5 minutes.

Mr. GARAMENDI. Thank you, Mr. Chairman.

A lot of things to discuss here. I think we are spending several billion dollars on a testing machine in Lawrence Livermore, aren't we, Dr. Anastasio? How is it working?

Dr. ANASTASIO. I believe you are talking about the National Ignition Facility, the NIF?

Mr. GARAMENDI. Oh, yes, that is what I am talking about. Dr.

ANASTASIO. I don't work at Lawrence Livermore anymore.

Mr. GARAMENDI. Well, I know you are familiar with it. You spent a lot of time teaching me about it, so——

Dr. ANASTASIO. Yes, sir. And it is good to see you, again, sir.

I think the Defense Science Board has looked at NIF and has felt it was a valuable tool and asset for the Stockpile Stewardship Program.

Mr. GARAMENDI. We will let it go at that.

Dr. ANASTASIO. I will say that much.

Mr. GARAMENDI. I think we need an update on that. It is an important element in what Mr. Lamborn just talked about.

I want to go to a recommendation here about tactical nuclear weapons. And under what circumstances does the Board assume that we would be using them?

Dr. JOHN. We were puzzled by the reference to us recommending tactical nuclear weapons, because we never wrote that. We just didn't say that.

Mr. GARAMENDI. Then how did I come to believe that you did? Maybe somebody is interpreting your work?

Dr. JOHN. Yes. I think somebody decided what we meant to say was.

Mr. GARAMENDI. What did you mean to say? Where are you with tactical nuclear weapons?

Dr. JOHN. If there is a military need, if the military stands up and says, we need it, then the enterprise will respond. But there is no military requirement right now.

Mr. GARAMENDI. Let me be sure that I understood. As far as the Board is concerned, you know of no military requirements for tactical nuclear weapons?

Dr. JOHN. Today.

Mr. GARAMENDI. Well, there is tomorrow.

Well, how about low-yield weapons, what is the purpose of a low-yield weapon?

Dr. ANASTASIO. Well, currently, without going into any detail here, we have weapon systems that have low yields.

Mr. GARAMENDI. Yes, we do.

Dr. ANASTASIO. As you know. And so they have a purpose. We have a requirement. The enterprise has a requirement to produce those, and that is fine.

I think the discussion that you have seen in this document was intended to be along the lines: We don't know what the future brings. We do see what adversaries are off doing. And I think the Board felt it was prudent for us to spend time thinking about how might we respond to a different requirement than we have today sometime in the future, would we be ready to respond to that?

Mr. GARAMENDI. In other words, do you have a low-yield tactical nuclear weapon?

Dr. ANASTASIO. Well, there are many, many different kinds of options that could be possible in the future and are we ready to be able to respond to that. So it is a capability question. It is not a recommendation that this is something that the country should be doing now. It is a desire to be capable of thinking about such a thing in the future.

Mr. GARAMENDI. Well, help me think about it for a while. We do have a nuclear weapon that has a quite low yield——

Dr. ANASTASIO. Yes, sir.

Mr. GARAMENDI [continuing]. And a quite high yield. Does that meet the anticipated—potential anticipated needs that you are thinking about? If not, why not?

Dr. ANASTASIO. Let's see, I am trying to think of how to answer that. We don't have a requirement for something other than that. So what might happen in the future is speculation.

I think what we are trying to—our intent was to distinguish between the technical capability of this enterprise versus the policy questions. We were not trying to address the policy questions of whether that is a good thing to do or an appropriate thing to do sometime in the future. It was more, are we as an enterprise collectively in the DOD and the DOE capable of responding to a different requirement than the ones we have today? And that is a technical capability question versus a statement about what the policy should be.

Mr. GARAMENDI. I am out of time. I will come back.

Mr. ROGERS. The Chair now recognizes the gentleman from Louisiana, Dr. Abraham, for 5 minutes.

Dr. ABRAHAM. Thank you, Mr. Chairman. I thank the witnesses for being here.

The DSB report from December emphasizes, and I am going to quote, "that the nuclear weapons are a steadily evolving threat," end of quote.

Would you please describe how the nuclear weapon threat has evolved, particularly since the last NPR [Nuclear Posture Review], I think what was written in 2010, the new threats, the new vulnerability, opportunities that have emerged are changed since that 2010 report?

Dr. JOHN. Let's see, we will be a little bit careful until we go into classified session, but certainly there is plenty of awareness in the public domain that Russia is fielding their modernized systems. They have been at it since the late 1990s to retool their capabilities. And that includes a number of advances in their air defense systems that present very thorny opportunity—I mean challenges for us to be able to penetrate Russian airspace.

In addition, the Chinese have gone from order a dozen strategic weapons, as in long-reach weapons, to something like 100 or so. And look at North Korea. We have underestimated them every step of the way. I will stop it at that.

Dr. ABRAHAM. Okay. And we will pick this up in a different briefing. That is all I have, Mr. Chairman. Thank you.

Mr. ROGERS. The Chair now recognizes Ms. Hanabusa for 5 minutes.

Ms. HANABUSA. Thank you, Mr. Chair. Thank you all for being here.

I think the problem that I am having with this is that when we talk about nuclear deterrence, you seem to imply in your report that there is both nuclear weapons, but also nonnuclear weapons that can also act as deterrents. And you talk about the triad, and we had a session yesterday where I was telling the military members who were sitting where you are that I think the assumption of the triad was something that I questioned right off the bat. In other words, how can you say something that has been in the shape that it has been for all these years, you talk about modernizations, which you also talk about, and then somehow the modernization includes the structure that has been there for all of these years.

13

So what I would like to ask you is, when you talk about the deterrence of nuclear weapons and you also mention the nonnuclear weapons, what are you talking about? And when you talk about modernizing the triad, it seems to assume that somehow the inherent structure of the triad is what we need. And I just can't understand how when you sit here before us that that would be something that you would begin this whole discussion with. So if anyone can take a stab at that.

Dr. LaPlante. I can start by saying the Board believes and enforces the fact that the triad needs to be strong, robust, and modernized. One would argue that we have used the—we use the triad every day, and we use the ICBMs [intercontinental ballistic missiles], we use the SSBNs [ballistic missile submarines] every day, we use the bombers every day, okay? We talked earlier about the fact that they are all running to the end of their life. And so what the Board has pointed out, as has others, is it is time to modernize.

Now, the triad itself is the ultimate part of deterrence. It is the ultimate. It is to deter the country against, God forbid, a nuclear attack. And the fact of the matter is there are other kinds of deterrence, lower on the escalation ladder, as you imply, conventional. But, God forbid, if all of those failed, all we have is the triad, and that is our point.

The other point about the triad is each leg of the triad has unique characteristics, and they are actually complementary with each other. The ICBMs, in order for an adversary to take out the ICBMs in a first strike, would have to be a massive first strike against the continental United States, something that would be a very high bar for any country, God forbid, to even think about, and that is what we want them, not to think about it.

The bombers have an inherent flexibility. We can signal with the bombers. We can move them. We can show them. We can recall them. They have a flexibility that is unique of themselves. The SSBNs are an ace in the hole. No matter what happens, they will always survive and be there as a credible second strike.

Now, there is always talk and there will be talk and there should be talk about is there a better way to do business. And we would encourage that. We think the NPR that is being started should be informed by the best experts. But the triad as I just described it and having it be modern and having been it be proficient and credible is the state that we are in, and that is what the Board emphasized in its report.

Ms. Hanabusa. So when the Board says it should be modern, I guess that is the problem I am having. I understand the SSBN. I understand the move from *Ohio* to *Columbia* class. That I understand. But when you talk about bombers or ICBMs, how do you modernize ICBMs?

And your other statement that I find curious, you say, we use it every day. How are we using ICBMs every day?

Dr. LaPlante. Right now there are people in the missile fields, in the LCCs [launch control centers], airmen in the LCCs, that are airmen doing that mission. So they are doing that mission right now as we speak.

Ms. Hanabusa. So are you saying we are deploying ICBMs every day?

Dr. LaPlante. No, the deterrence posture—we have right now SSBNs in the ocean, we have ICBMs in CONUS [continental United States], in the United States, and we have bombers. Those are all part of an active deterrent that operates 24/7.

Ms. Hanabusa. So when you say we are using it every day, you are not meaning we are actually using it in the conventional sense. You mean just their presence is sufficient to be the deterrent?

Dr. LaPlante. Absolutely. Absolutely.

Dr. Anastasio. Absolutely.

Dr. LaPlante. In fact, that is the point. The point is, you know, there are the three C's of deterrence: credibility, capability, and clarity. And this is part of the capability. We have to show that we have this capability.

Ms. Hanabusa. My time is almost up, so we will continue this in the next session.

Dr. LaPlante. Sure.

Ms. Hanabusa. I yield back, Mr. Chair.

Mr. Rogers. I thank the gentlelady. The Chair now recognizes the gentleman from Colorado, Mr. Coffman, for 5 minutes.

Mr. Coffman. Thank you, Mr. Chairman.

When we talk about the triad, I am awfully concerned about the next-generation bomber. And given our capability in terms of cruise missiles, of precision guidance, guided munitions, those things, how important is it to have—I mean, is that part of the triad in terms of having a next-generation manned bomber? Is that dated or is that still as critical as it has always been?

Dr. LaPlante. The Board has not, as far as I know, actually— the Defense Science Board has not addressed that specific question. I have personal experience in this in my previous job as the Assistant Secretary of the Air Force, but the Board has not answered that.

But I would say that it is a policy of the United States and the plan that the next bomber, the B–21, is replacing and is that part of the triad. And as the Air Force has stated publicly, initially it is going to be manned, but they are building in the hooks and the capabilities, so if there is a potential future that it needs to be un- manned they don't have to start from scratch.

Mr. Coffman. Okay.

"Redundancy" is a term we hear repeatedly when discussing the nuclear triad and our ability to retaliate in the event of a hostile nuclear attack. How vulnerable are our satellite detection systems to Chinese and Russian kinetic kill or directed energy antisatellite weapons? Are these systems redundant in any way?

Dr. LaPlante. I will try to answer it, because the Board has looked at space, and there is a limited amount we can say in this open session. But are you saying is the triad redundant given anti- space capabilities?

Mr. Coffman. That is right, ASAT [antisatellite] capability.

Dr. LaPlante. By an adversary?

Mr. Coffman. Right.

Dr. LaPlante. No. No, it is not. In fact, quite the contrary. The idea being that these—like, I used the example of the SSBNs and others. We have to have ways that the triad can be a credible de- terrent even in the most extreme warfighting scenario, and including in a space situation. So while we can't go into the details here, a nuclear command and control has to be robust enough to deal with the fact that space is going to also be contested, so communications that use space have to be considered redundancies, resiliencies to deal with that to make sure the triad works.

But, no, no. In fact, the triad is supposed to be able to be robust against the full spectrum of space threats, cyber threats, and, God forbid, a nuclear threat.

Mr. COFFMAN. Thank you, Mr. Chairman. I yield back.

Mr. ROGERS. The Chair now recognizes the gentleman from California, Mr. Khanna, for 5 minutes.

Mr. KHANNA. Thank you, Mr. Chair.

Do you agree with President Ronald Reagan's statement that a nuclear war cannot be won and must never be fought?

Dr. ANASTASIO. I think it is the hope of all of us that we never have a nuclear war.

Mr. KHANNA. That wasn't his statement. He said it must never be fought. I mean, it can't be won. Do you believe that he was correct, or do you believe that we need to reconsider President Reagan's approach to deal with nuclear weapons because the times have changed? And do you think that—are you here saying that his thinking is outdated, or do you believe that his thinking still applies?

Dr. ANASTASIO. I don't know if I could speak for the Board in that regard.

Dr. JOHN. Let's see, let me help Mike out a little bit. That is a policy statement which we, representing the Defense Science Board, really would act upon or not.

We will say that we start with prevent nuclear war, and the foundation for that is deterrence. And as I believe one of your briefers said yesterday, and I can't remember who it was, or General Kehler might have said in different testimony, that the paradox of deterrence is that they have to be convinced that you actually would use it. We have devoted our lives to putting substance behind that proposition, and if you think there is a better way to do deterrence, I think we would love to hear it.

Mr. KHANNA. I guess I want to get your views in terms of—I mean, I think President Reagan—and I disagreed with him on so many things, but I think that many people would say that he had an aspiration for peace. He, if you read his biographies, said that he never wanted to see nuclear war. That is why he came up with Star Wars, whatever you may think of it.

And my question is just he clearly would disagree with what you are proposing, at least from his public statement. So are you rejecting President Reagan's legacy on this issue? Which would be fine, I mean, you can say we are in different times and President Reagan didn't know what he was talking about when it came to nuclear deterrence and you have a different approach. I just want to see if that is your view.

Dr. JOHN. I don't know how different it is today, because the most significant modernization program, last modernization program, was in his administration, modernization of our nuclear weapons.

Dr. LaPlante. We are living off the modernization, many of which was done during the Reagan administration, the *Ohio* class, the Minuteman. And so, again, the Defense Science Board is not a policy board.

Now, clearly, the objective of having a triad as a deterrent is stability. And stability is, as I my colleague here said, is what you are after. You are after stability. You are after stability. And the paradox is to get stability in deterrence theory, you have to have a credible capability. That is the paradox.

Mr. KHANNA. I guess I still want to just get to the point. I agree with your point on modernization having been done there, but your quote, which is in the Defense Science Board's report, that you believe in a more flexible nuclear enterprise for limited use, that basically what you are saying is that we should have a first strike option if it is in our strategic interest. Is that not correct? I mean, because that is how Senator Feinstein characterized it in her op-ed this morning.

Dr. ANASTASIO. I would suggest that that is not what we—what the Board believes. What we believe is—as my colleague said, we are not making policy recommendations. What we are trying to say, is in an uncertain future, are we capable and prepared to respond in whatever way the policy makers in this country decide we should? Are we prepared, are we capable, can we go execute that if that were something that was required of the community?

And that is one of the things that we believe has been ignored in recent decades, which is, how do you think about what potential things you might have to do in the future and how do you assure the country and our adversaries that if this country has to go a different place, that we are ready to go there and capable of doing that?

And so it is not making a policy recommendation that we should do this or should do that, and I think that is a misreading of our report.

Mr. ROGERS. The gentleman's time has expired.

The Chair now recognizes the gentlelady from Wyoming, Ms. Cheney, for 5 minutes.

Ms. CHENEY. Thank you, Mr. Chairman.

I want to take issue with my colleague from California's interpretation of Ronald Reagan's policy. You know, President Reagan believed and said that war comes not when the forces of freedom are strong, it is actually when we are weak that we are threatened.

So wouldn't you say that fundamental to the notion that nuclear war should never be fought is the idea that our forces must, in fact, be so strong, so able to overwhelm any adversary that they understand they will not survive such a conflict? That, in fact, deterrence requires both a characterization and calculation about the threats we face, but also ensuring the lethality, the modernization, the effectiveness of our force across a broad array of circumstances so that our adversaries never mistake any action that we take for some sort of indication that they could actually prevail in a nuclear conflict?

Dr. ANASTASIO. Yeah, it is a risk-benefit. It is, does an adversary believe that if they take an action that they would gain more benefit than they would have to pay a cost in our response?

And I think my comment, back to the previous question, was along that line, is how do we make sure an adversary believes that whatever avenue they try to follow to negate the military capability of this country, whatever avenue they pursue, that we are ready and capable of responding in whatever way we have to, to convince them that whatever benefit they think they might accrue, that is not going to work, and that we can impose a cost that is much more significant than the benefit they think they can gain.

Dr. LaPlante. I would just add that the classic deterrence theory is, this is the hardest part, is you are really trying to get—all that matters is inside the head of the adversary or peer that you are trying to deter. And so, as my colleague said, the idea behind deterrence, the theory of deterrence is fundamental, is that, as you said, whatever action that this adversary, potential adversary, is going to take to their advantage, that they must be convinced that the downside of taking that action will way overrule any upside they will get. That is the theory.

Ms. Cheney. Thank you. And I think it is important also just for the record to point out that it was the policy of President Reagan to ensure that we had superiority across the Board, including in our nuclear forces, so that, in fact, we could guarantee that nuclear war would never be fought.

I yield back, Mr. Chairman.

Mr. Rogers. All right. The Chair now recognizes the ranking member.

Mr. Larsen. Thank you, Mr. Chairman. I would just ask consent to enter into the record the January 11 statement from Roy Schwitters and the January 11 letter from Richard Garwin, both with regards to Peer Review and Design Competition in the NNSA [National Nuclear Security Administration] National Security Laboratories.

Mr. Rogers. Without objection, so ordered.

[The information referred to can be found in the Appendix beginning on page 41.]

Mr. Rogers. We are now going to stand in recess as we move to—what room are we moving to? To another room. We are in recess.

[Whereupon, at 4:31 p.m., the subcommittee proceeded in closed session.]

APPENDIX

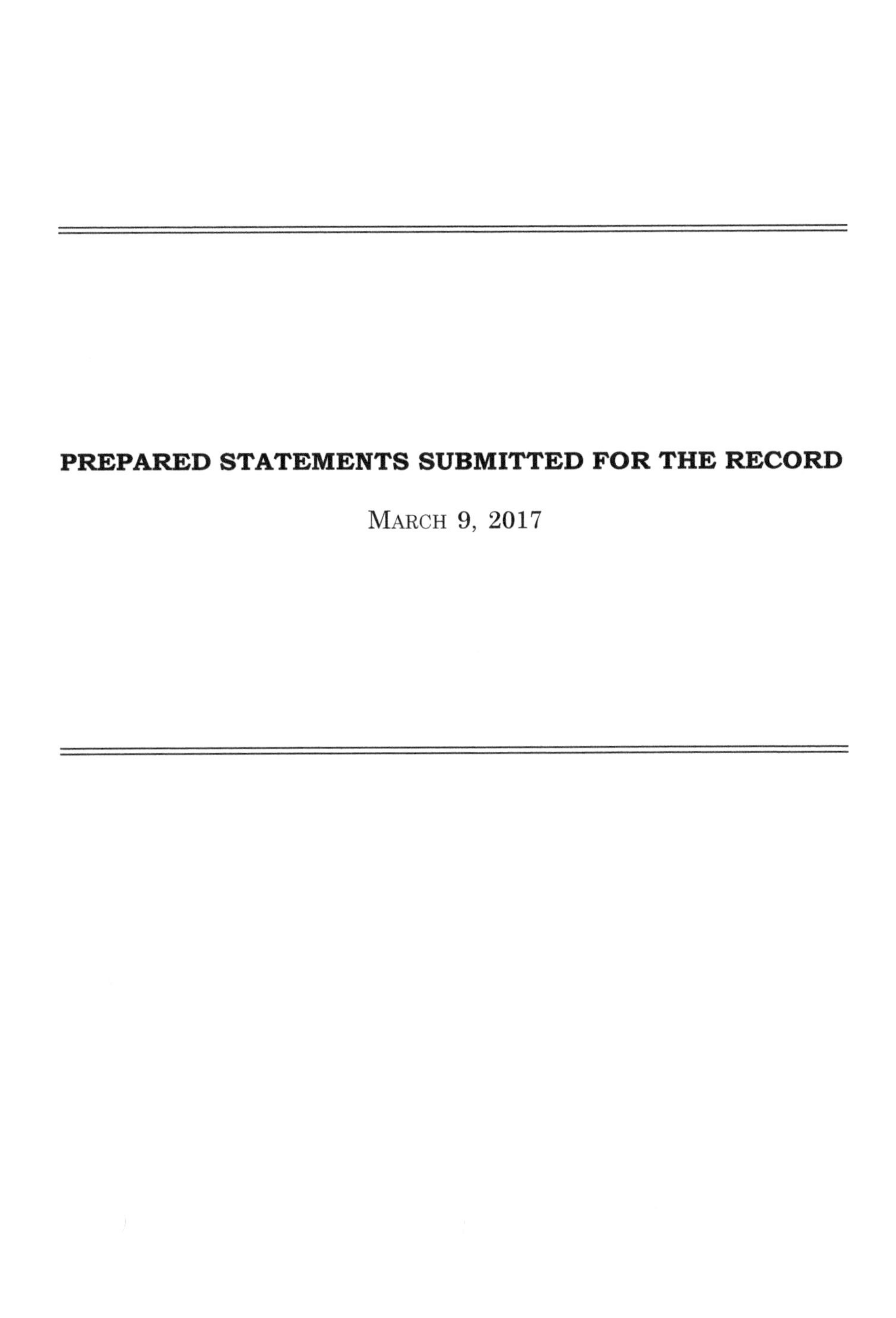

PREPARED STATEMENTS SUBMITTED FOR THE RECORD

MARCH 9, 2017

Opening Remarks – As Prepared for Delivery
The Honorable Mike Rogers
Chairman, Subcommittee on Strategic Forces
House Armed Services Committee

Hearing on the "Nuclear Deterrence—the Defense Science Board's Perspective"
March 9, 2017

Good afternoon. The subcommittee will come to order.

Welcome to our hearing on "Nuclear Deterrence—the Defense Science Board's Perspective."

I want to thank our witnesses for being here today and for your service to the public.

Our witnesses are all experts who have spent their careers in fields related to nuclear deterrence. They are appearing today in their capacities as Members of the Defense Science Board, but all have long and distinguished histories in the topic of our hearing.

We thank you for the hard work it takes to prepare for this hearing. Our witnesses are:

- Dr. Michael Anastasio
- Dr. Miriam John
- Dr. William LaPlante

In December 2016, in the waning days of the Obama Administration, the Defense Science Board completed a report titled "Seven Defense Priorities for the New Administration." It made recommendations to the new Trump Administration on key issues in the world of defense.

Chapter 2 of this report summarized years of work by the Board on nuclear deterrence. Which is exactly what we will explore today.

The Board has published 12 studies over the past 14 years on this topic. So it's clear the Board has spent a lot of time thinking about this.

As well it should: a defense mission of such importance seems worthy of sustained and focused attention. And our military and civilian defense leaders have repeatedly said nuclear deterrence is our highest priority defense mission.

We heard this very clearly just yesterday from the Vice Chairman of the Joint Chiefs of Staff and other senior military officers.

As the new Administration and Congress goes forward with the nuclear modernization program initiated by President Obama, we should take stock of where we and other nuclear powers are at—and where we're going.

The Board's report correctly notes that "nuclear weapons are a steadily evolving threat—in both new and familiar directions." We must understand how the threat is evolving and anticipate what must be done to compensate.

Of course, we must also understand where we've been. The Board notes that the "after 25 years of downplaying (and poorly resourcing) the mission" significant investment is needed to ensure a credible nuclear deterrent.

Importantly, the Board notes that despite the U.S. focus on downplaying the utility of nuclear weapons, many other nations have not done the same.

Our witnesses today will be able to provide the collective views and recommendations of the Board, as well as their own views as Board Members.

Informing the public is a big part of our job up here, and the American people need to hear from independent experts like you on where we should be going with our nuclear deterrent.

Directly after this hearing, the subcommittee will meet in a closed session to continue the discussion with our witnesses at a classified level. Members must understand the sensitive details of both foreign threats and U.S. capabilities to fully appreciate the Board's assessment.

Ensuring a credible nuclear deterrent—for the long-term future—will continue to be a major priority for this nation, this Congress, and this Committee.

As Chairman Thornberry said yesterday: "this hearing and the Committee's broader series on nuclear deterrence will remind us, the American people, our allies, and our potential adversaries that the U.S. strategic deterrent must always be credible and must always be ready."

# # #

Statement by Hon. Rick Larsen
Strategic Forces Subcommittee Hearing
Nuclear Deterrence—The Defense Science Board's Perspective
March 9, 2017

Drs. Anastasio, John, and LaPlante, I join Chairman Rogers in welcoming you to this hearing on nuclear deterrence.

Ranking Member Cooper is unable to participate in today's hearing, but he also thanks you for joining us today.

As independent advisors, the Defense Science Board has an important role to play in making recommendations on scientific and technical matters to DOD leadership.

In its "Seven Defense Priorities for the New Administration" report, the DSB correctly noted that our nuclear forces remain a cornerstone of U.S. national security.

I agree that this is one of the most important areas for the Department and our committee to focus.

Given how critical these nuclear systems are, and with costly modernization programs occurring concurrently, we cannot afford to get this wrong.

While I appreciate the vision represented in this report, I would be remiss if I did not mention that DOD has still been unable to provide a 30-year estimate on the full costs of nuclear modernization.

This is not a matter of partisan politics. Members of the committee have been asking for this accounting across multiple administrations.

In your report, you write that the budget for modernization "will significantly compromise investments in conventional capabilities."

This commonsense observation should alarm those who seek to downplay the impact on the defense budget of nuclear modernization, and provoke all of us to understand the inherent trade-offs that are looming.

There are other elements of this report I find concerning.

You recommend prototyping and fielding new low-yield nuclear weapons.

I found the justification to be unclear. Are these intended to address new threats? To enable us to reduce our stockpile of other types of nuclear weapons? To deter a Russian "escalate-to-deescalate" scenario? To keep nuclear weapons scientists sharp and interested in their mission?

These are very different objectives, and I have not seen any sufficiently detailed analysis of what the proposals are, whether these proposals are necessary, what alternatives are being considered, what the trade-offs are, what the cost would be, and what the policy implications are.

And I find this recommendation to run contrary to General Hyten's testimony yesterday. During our full committee hearing, General Hyten stated that deployment of nuclear weapons is always an attempt to achieve strategic effects, and disagreed with the distinction between "tactical" and "strategic" nuclear weapons.

Smaller nuclear weapons would require prototyping. However, Dr. Richard Garwin and Dr. Roy Schwitters, both of the eminent JASONs scientific group, strongly criticized the need and value of manufacturing prototypes of new nuclear weapons in written comments to this subcommittee last year.

I am particularly concerned that new types of nuclear weapons would have significant policy and proliferation implications.

Adding new military capability and building new nuclear weapons would be a radical shift, one that Congress—rightly so—has not been willing to approve for nearly 25 years.

This approach could lead to a requirement for renewed nuclear testing, a policy shift that would be unwise, unnecessary and have potentially disastrous consequences in re-legitimizing nuclear testing and helping to advance our adversaries' nuclear forces.

The DSB report more explicitly opens the door to the potential need to resume testing. Until now and for the foreseeable future, our top scientists have confirmed that there is no need to resume nuclear testing to certify the current nuclear stockpile.

Still, there is much to commend in your report.

It highlights, correctly I believe, the need for investments in detection and monitoring technologies which can reduce the threat posed by nuclear proliferation.

With new technologies such as 3-D printing emerging, these investments can support current and future nonproliferation and arms control agreements with a robust technological foundation.

The report also correctly identifies some of the geopolitical complexities that have challenged our nuclear deterrent. These include proliferation of nuclear weapons and our allies concerns that the U.S. may be weakening its security guarantees.

As a candidate, President Trump expressed support for proliferation and threatened the sanctity of American security guarantees to our allies.

It is my sincere hope that as Commander-in-Chief, he understands the destabilizing effect of these statements.

A 2014 DSB report warned that, "For the first time since the early decades of the nuclear era, the nation needs to be equally concerned about both "vertical" proliferation (the increase in capabilities of existing nuclear states) and "horizontal" proliferation (an increase in the number of states and non-state actors possessing or attempting to possess nuclear weapons)...

monitoring for proliferation should be a top national security objective—but one for which the nation is not yet organized or fully equipped to address."

Your comments and insights on this issue are most welcome and I would be interested in more specific recommendations in support of this mission, particularly with regard to what gaps remain and how we can use advancing technology and analytic approaches, including big data analytics, to improve our capabilities.

Thank you for joining us today.

###

**Testimony before the
House Armed Services Subcommittee on Strategic Forces
by Dr. Miriam John, Dr. Michael Anastasio, and Dr. William LaPlante
March 9, 2017**

Introduction

Chairman Rogers, Ranking Member Cooper, and members of the Subcommittee, we thank
you for the opportunity to testify today concerning "Nuclear Deterrence – the Defense Science
Board's Perspective". We will present and discuss the principal findings and
recommendations developed by the Defense Science Board (DSB) over the past ~15 years on
topics related to nuclear deterrence. These results are summarized in Chapter 2 of the recently
published DSB report "Seven Defense Priorities for the New Administration."

Background on the DSB

First, however, we want to introduce the members of the subcommittee to the DSB, since we
understand that some of you may not be familiar with the organization. The Board was
established as a Federal Advisory Committee in 1956 as an independent source of scientific
and technical advice to the Secretary of Defense and his/her leadership team, both civilian and
military.

The Board today consists of 46 members, all of whom give their time pro bono, and devote
upwards of 60 days a year. Members include senior executives from defense and commercial
industry; retired flag officers; former senior officials from DoD, the State Department, and the
Intelligence Community; university professors; and leaders of Federally Funded Research and
Development Centers (FFRDCs) and National Laboratories. Many are members of the
National Academies of Science, Engineering, and Medicine. Collectively we bring a strong
background and interest in science and technology, and deep knowledge of DoD, national
security, and the Federal Government so that our recommendations are realistic and can be
implemented.

We are tasked by Department leadership in OSD, and occasionally by Congress, with
difficult, unstructured problems for which solutions might address high consequence issues or
present game changing opportunities. A few examples to illustrate the range of our activities
over those 60 years include:

- *"Owning the Night" – achieving night vision*
- *Design of a U.S. Anti-Satellite capability*

- *Concept for Assault Breaker, which led to the Army's Tactical Missile System(ATACMS)*
- *Secretary Directive 3000.05 Military Support for Stability, Security, Transition and Reconstruction Operations*
- *"Submarine of the Future" - the design of fast attack submarines*
- *Electronic Warfare*
- *Strategic Surprise (What are we neglecting in 2014 that we will regret in 2024?)*
- *Autonomy's potential as part of the "third offset"*

We are expected to be persistent on matters we think critical, such as cyber, where we can point to more than a 20-year recognition of vulnerabilities and therefore threats, and evolving recommendations on what to do. Of interest to this subcommittee would be the near continuous attention given to nuclear issues throughout the 60-year history of the board, including a successive string of task forces in the past 15 years during a time, until recently, when nuclear issues assumed a lower profile in national and Department priorities.

The three of us represent more than 100 years of experience in nuclear weapon and broader national security matters. Dr. Anastasio had a 31-year career with DOE's nuclear weapons design laboratories, having served as Director of Lawrence Livermore National Laboratory and following that, as Director of Los Alamos National Laboratory. He is a 5-year member of the DSB and is in his 14th-year supporting the Commander of Strategic Command (STRATCOM) as a STRATCOM Advisory Group (SAG) member and a special advisor. Dr. John spent 28 years associated with nuclear weapons systems engineering at Sandia National Laboratories, retiring as Director of its California Laboratory, and is a 13-year member of the DSB, as well as Vice Chairman of DoD's Threat Reduction Advisory Committee. Both have been recruited and continue to stay involved in nuclear related matters after retiring from their laboratory positions. Dr. LaPlante has worked with nuclear delivery systems since 1985, led the Fleet Ballistic Submarine (SSBN) Security Program at the Johns Hopkins Applied Physics Laboratory, and has been a STRATCOM SAG special advisor for 11 years. Most recently Dr. LaPlante served for approximately three years as the Assistant Secretary of the Air Force for Acquisition where he oversaw nuclear modernization programs such as Ground Based Strategic Deterrent (GBSD) and the B-21 bomber. He too continues to be involved in nuclear related issues as a Vice President of the MITRE Corporation.

<u>The DSB's Perspectives on Nuclear Deterrence</u>

With that as background, we will now focus on the DSB's "Seven Defense Priorities for the New Administration." The purpose of this effort was to present the DSB's perspective on the most pressing national security issues and opportunities to the incoming Administration to help them in making a fast start. While the topics that have been addressed by the DSB span a wide range, seven major themes dominated the Board's considerations. Today we will discuss the theme relevant to this hearing "Deterring the Use of Nuclear Weapons".

Key Elements of Nuclear Deterrence

There is no more important objective than preventing a nuclear attack on the United States or its allies. The strategy for prevention has rested on deterring an attack by making the cost to the adversary who would dare so high that it outweighs any perceived benefit so that he would never attack in the first place. The realization of that strategy has evolved to three principal elements, which are manifest in the U.S.' nuclear forces, the so-called Triad:

1. Strategic (ongoing) stability: through single warhead intercontinental ballistic missiles; i.e., the adversary would have to commit to a massive, pre-emptive attack on the continental U.S. to negate that capability;
2. Crisis stability and flexibility: through an air delivered force; i.e., bombers and fighters carrying nuclear weapons with a longer execution time than a ballistic missile and which could be deployed worldwide;
3. Assured second strike: through submarine-launched ballistic missiles; i.e., a system difficult to detect and always on patrol.

The DSB believes that the Triad's complementary features remain robust tenets for the design of a future force. Replacing our current, aging force is essential, but not sufficient in the more complex nuclear environment we now face to provide the adaptability or flexibility to confidently hold at risk what adversaries value. In particular, if the threat evolves in ways that favorably change the cost/benefit calculus in the view of an adversary's leadership, then we should be in a position to quickly restore a credible deterrence posture.

While the Triad represents the most visible manifestation of deterrence and is overdue for modernization, there are many other factors that contribute to deterrence and also require attention. Together with the Triad, these factors present to any adversary the credibility that the U.S. is fully capable of executing against our strategy under any circumstance; namely that the U.S. can impose unacceptable costs and/or negate any perceived benefits of an adversary's actions. They include:

- The operational readiness of the force as demonstrated through training and exercises;
- The ability and capacity of the technical enterprise to anticipate and respond to changes in the threat;
- The ability to operate in an adversary generated nuclear environment (referred to as nuclear survivability);
- A robust command and control system;
- Preventing further proliferation – both "vertically" by current nuclear weapons actors, and "horizontally" by new proliferators – through the tools of diplomacy (treaties and

agreements), cooperative and unilateral monitoring, and assurance/extended deterrence to our allies.
- The lynchpin: the demonstrated skills of talented, knowledgeable, committed, and valued people.

The DSB has addressed each of these areas (with the exception of command and control, a topic covered by special commissions) in some depth throughout its history, and especially over the past 15 years as we began to see worrisome trends in the threat..

The Evolving Threat

Despite the "peace dividend" at the end of the Cold War, the DSB remained unconvinced that downplaying the nation's nuclear deterrent would lead other nations to do the same, even as advances in the U.S.' non-nuclear warfighting capabilities proved their effectiveness.
In fact, U.S. conventional dominance demonstrated in Bosnia, Iraq, and Afghanistan, as well as regional imperatives, appears to have catalyzed a greater interest in nuclear weapons by others who do not have the resources to overmatch the U.S. otherwise. The DSB has therefore maintained steady attention on the health of the U.S. nuclear enterprise, Russian and Chinese efforts to advance and modernize their nuclear arsenals, proliferation by other nation states, and advances in technology that could both detect and hide proliferation. The collection of findings point to a worrisome conclusion: the nuclear threshold may be decreasing owing to the stated doctrines and weapons developments of some states, and with introduction of new technology.

The threat from nuclear weapons has grown in ways not experienced during the Cold War. Established nuclear powers modernized and expanded their capabilities in both traditional and non-traditional ways. Both China and Russia began modernizing their strategic forces well ahead of the U.S.' commitment to do the same, while also integrating additional elements such as intermediate range missiles and integrated air defenses, into their force structure. China's nuclear efforts focus on a survivable second-strike force, complemented by non-nuclear capabilities that match or offset U.S. non-nuclear forces and networked operations. In addition to its strategic force modernization, Russia embarked on a steady path since the late 1990s of conventional improvements in precision, stealth, and speed, and development and deployment of theater nuclear weapons with a range of tailored effects in response to U.S. conventional superiority. The Department has seen the relentless pursuit of nuclear capabilities to threaten the homeland by the Democratic People's Republic of Korea, the recently halted march to acquisition by Iran, and the talk of proliferation by some non-nuclear allies and partners who are questioning the U.S.' commitment to extended deterrence and security guarantees. Commerce in the sale or sharing of nuclear materials and weapons design appeared, and advances in technologies readily accessible even to non-state actors introduce new pathways to acquisition.

Although the threat of nuclear Armageddon has subsided, the nation must still hedge against the existential risk of a massive nuclear exchange, no matter how slim. However, the threats of proliferation, the potential for the U.S. weakening assurance guarantees of its allies, and the emerging scenarios of limited use in regional conflicts or limited strike against the U.S. homeland—with the potential for escalation—introduce complexities not seen since the early days of the Cold War. To address these complexities, U.S. policy has evolved to seek to raise the threshold for nuclear use, at least by the U.S., by relying less on nuclear forces and more on our advanced non-nuclear capabilities, while also committing to modernizing those nuclear force elements deemed critical for deterrence against a massive exchange.

US Nuclear Force and Enterprise Modernization

Nuclear force modernization has been put off far too long. The looming end-of-life of the Triad components and aging production infrastructure is forcing both the DoD and the DOE to commit substantial resources to nuclear modernization. The lead time for obtaining a modernized force is long and the U.S. is starting well behind Russian and Chinese efforts. A balanced program to support the nuclear deterrent force capabilities would consist of three elements: (1) certification and maintenance of current systems; (2) life extension of current systems, and replacement of those systems that can no longer be maintained to the required levels of reliability, safety, and security; and (3) a hedging thrust for responding to future uncertainties. For the first two decades after the end of the Cold War, the U.S. remained unbalanced among the three as attention was paid almost exclusively to sustaining the existing stockpile. Attention to the second element has grown only with the "impossible to ignore" reality in the last few years of end-of-life of critical platforms and warheads. The uptick in priority for nuclear force modernization in both DoD and DOE sends a strong message of U.S. commitment to the deterrent that must continue.

There is still no clearly identifiable set of activities that address the third element, a convincing hedge to future uncertainties, nor has there been since the early 1990s. Already the DoD can anticipate the potential need for capabilities such as a robust nuclear command and control network; hardening or maneuvering for defense penetration; command and control to target to allow command disable in flight should a limited strike scenario not evolve as anticipated; real time battle damage assessment; and embedded weapon system state-of-health monitoring for greater assurance of reliable functioning of a given weapon should a limited use option be necessary. To rapidly field such capabilities would require a production capability utilizing state-of-the-art manufacturing techniques, weapon system architectures, and certification strategies that could support block changes or "plug-and-play" components.

However, there are challenges to overcome to enable a convincing hedge to future uncertainties. A key contributor to nuclear deterrence is the continuous, adaptable exercise of the development, design, and production functions for nuclear weapons in both the DoD and DOE. The DOE principally manages warhead development and production. The DoD's roles are equally critical in setting system requirements, synchronizing the development, production, and adaptation of the delivery platform, and setting the weapon-platform interface requirements. Yet the DOE laboratories and DoD contractor community have done little integrated design and development work outside of life extension for 25 years, let alone concept development that could serve as a hedge to surprise. They are ramping up their efforts to address modernization schedules, but of necessity the new workforce contains a large fraction of inexperienced scientists and especially engineers. And in DOE especially, the ramp up is occurring in facilities well beyond their lifetime and with limited capacity that will stretch schedules to 2040. Plans for facility recapitalization compete with warhead life extension and modernization programs. The last successful construction of a new nuclear component production facility was in 1976. The DoD platform modernization requirements are occurring almost simultaneously with DOE's programs and also extend over two decades, challenged in its case by competing modernization and recapitalization demands for the conventional force.

Nuclear Survivability

If U.S. nuclear forces are to be part of a credible deterrent, they must be able to survive and function in a nuclear environment. A thornier issue is how to maintain our conventional superiority and keep our own nuclear threshold as high as possible in the face of an adversary's limited regional use of his own nuclear weapons. Our critical non-nuclear forces must be able to "fight through" in such a nuclear environment if we seek to rely on those forces as part of our deterrent posture, as has been the desire of successive administrations since the end of the Cold War. In almost all cases in the post Cold War era, however, the attention paid to the topic of nuclear survivability has been limited, in part because of beliefs until recently that theater nuclear use was not a risk, in part because of perceptions that the only recourse is equipment hardening and that the cost to harden is prohibitive, and in part because of the atrophy in the specialized knowledge in nuclear weapons effects and nuclear warfighting principles associated with survivability.

The DSB's persistence on this topic from 2005-2015 ran in parallel and beyond the two phases of the prior Electromagnetic Pulse (EMP) Commission, and resulted not only in a series of reports, but a gradual shift that has started to occur with formal directives and reporting to periodically assess the status of deployed force elements and to ensure that nuclear survivability is addressed in the requirements for major new acquisitions. But progress will necessarily be slow for developing a new generation of nuclear savvy acquirers, planners, and operators. The DSB has recommended a concerted and systematic approach based on the principle of mission assurance, not equipment hardening, in which:

- Combatant Commands identify mission critical functions derived from operational plans and Military Services then devolve that to mission critical capabilities;
- The analytical community provides support to link mission critical capabilities to specific systems and tactics, techniques, and procedures (TTPs);
- The operational community conducts gaming and experimentation in radiation degraded environments to identify gaps and uncertainties that are subsequently addressed;
- The Military Services ensure a tiered system of education and training in nuclear warfighting, to include a "101" level of knowledge throughout the force and among decision makers;
- The acquisition community sets requirements and the testing and evaluation community conduct assessments tied to mission assurance, not simply hardening levels.
- The technical community is regrown to support all of these activities.

Deterring Acquisition

Another aspect of deterrence has always been limiting the number of nations possessing nuclear weapons (nonproliferation) and for those that do, limiting the numbers and types in their arsenals (arms control). A major DSB effort associated with this area concluded that any progress in treaties and agreements had to take into account the compounding complexities that appear to be aggravating nuclear proliferation concerns into the foreseeable future:

- rogue state actions, such as those of the Democratic People's Republic of Korea, and the potential cascading effects on neighboring allies or partners;
- the impact of advancing technologies relevant to nuclear weapons development;
- the evidence of networks of cooperation among countries that would otherwise have little reason to do so;
- the implications of U.S. policy that relies more heavily on conventional military superiority as a major element of deterrence, accompanied by reductions in numbers of our nuclear weapons;
- the wide range of motivations, capabilities, and approaches that each potential proliferator introduces; i.e., it's no longer just about Russia.

In such a context, the DSB observed that the technical approach for monitoring cannot continue to derive only from treaty and agreement dictates for "point" compliance to the numbers and types formally agreed upon and geographically bounded. Monitoring in this future context must be a continuous process for which persistent surveillance tailored to the environment of concern is needed. This leads to the need for a paradigm shift in which the boundaries are blurred between monitoring for compliance and monitoring for proliferation, between cooperative and unilateral measures. Monitoring will need to be continuous, adaptive, and frequently tested for its effectiveness against an array of differing, creative and equally adaptive proliferators. In order to create such a comprehensive monitoring framework, three key elements would be needed:

- A systems analytical "white team" able to posit alternative futures, assess current capabilities to detect proliferation, identify gaps and evaluate alternatives;
- New tools to enable proliferation detection as early as possible to achieve persistent monitoring over widespread geographic areas for long periods of time, along with the data analytic capabilities to sift through the massive data sets generated;
- A red-blue field testing capability to elucidate the signatures for proliferation involved with small programs, denial and deception, advanced technologies, etc.

Deeper looks into the early detection problem suggest that there is as yet untapped potential in open source monitoring, making use of state-of-the-art techniques in "big data" analytics for cueing more sophisticated and precise collection resources.

<u>Summary</u>

The level of interest in nuclear weapons has grown with existing nuclear powers, who are modernizing their forces, and in some cases, expanding their capabilities both qualitatively and quantitatively, and with new or latent proliferators. Principal drivers include an affordable hedge against U.S. conventional superiority and a deterrent against regional actors that threaten their interests or sovereignty. In parallel, an aging nuclear force and enterprise to support it in the U.S. has forced the need for a modernization program of our own. The nation, DoD and DOE are stepping up to the commitment needed for modernization (with more focus required to hedging for future uncertainties), but the price to pay in both human resources and budget is substantial, given the more than two decades of neglect. Through its persistence over those decades, the DSB has produced a compendium of findings and recommendations across the spectrum of contributors to deterrence that can provide a rapid head start for the re-learning that must take place.

Dr. Miriam E. John

Dr. Miriam E. John is serving in various consulting and board roles since her retirement as Vice President of Sandia's California Laboratory in Livermore, California. During her Sandia career, she worked on a wide variety of programs, including nuclear weapons, chemical and biological defense, missile defense, solar energy, and provided leadership for a number of the laboratory's energy, national security, and homeland security programs.

She is a member of the DoD's Defense Science Board (DSB) and Vice Chairman of its Threat Reduction Advisory Committee (TRAC). She is also a member of the AAAS Committee on Science and Engineering Public Policy (COSEPP) and serves as Vice Chairman of the Board of Directors of the National Institute for Hometown Security. She is the immediate past Chair of the National Research Council's Naval Studies Board, a member of its Intelligence Science and Technology Experts Group and its Board on Chemical Sciences and Technology.

Dr. John is a member of the Board of Advisors for MIT Lincoln Laboratory, the Board of Directors for Sandia National Laboratories and for the Charles Stark Draper Laboratory, and the Board of Directors of Leidos, Inc. (formerly SAIC). She has recently been recruited as a member of the Mission Committee of the combined Lawrence Livermore and Los Alamos National Laboratories' Board, overseeing the technical programs of both laboratories. She is a Senior Fellow and immediate past Chair of the California Council on Science and Technology. Dr. John is a member of the Dean's advisory board for the School of Science and Engineering and chairs the Advisory Board for the Department of Chemical and Biomolecular Engineering at Tulane University, where she has been recognized as an outstanding alumna. She is a member of the External Advisory Board of the DOE sponsored, UC Berkeley led National Science and Security Consortium.

She was appointed a National Associate of the National Academies of Science and Engineering and is the recipient of the Navy's Superior Public Service Award. She was named the 2015 recipient of DoD's Eugene G. Fubini Award for her "significant and sustained contributions in an advisory capacity to the Department."

Mike Anastasio

Dr. Michael R. Anastasio is currently serving on the Defense Department Defense Science Board, as a Special Advisor to the Commander of the United States Strategic Command, as a Member of the Corporation of the Draper Laboratory, as a Member of the Board of Governors for Los Alamos National Security, LLC and Lawrence Livermore National Security, LLC, as a Member of the Secretary of Energy's Advisory Board Task Force on the National Laboratories, and as a member of the National Academy of Sciences Committee on Peer Review and Design Competition in the NNSA National Security Laboratories. He has also served on other boards and committees including the State Department International Security Advisory Board, the Congressional Advisory Panel on the Governance of the Nuclear Security Enterprise, the National Academy of Sciences Committee on Science & Technology for Countering Terrorism, the California Council on Science and Technology, and the Blue Ribbon Task Force on Nanotechnology.

Dr. Anastasio is the former Director of Los Alamos National Laboratory (LANL), retiring in 2011. LANL applies science and technology to the certification of the U.S. nuclear deterrent; the reduction of global threats; advancing energy security; and the solution of other emerging national security challenges. Dr. Anastasio is also the former Director of Lawrence Livermore National Laboratory (LLNL), the only person to ever hold both positions.

He began his career at LLNL as a physicist dealing with the science of nuclear weapons. During his tenure Dr. Anastasio was instrumental in the development and execution of the national Stockpile Stewardship Program, which uses fundamental science-based approach to sustain the safety, security, and reliability of America's nuclear weapons stockpile. He has served in the capacity of scientific adviser at the Department of Energy and has provided scientific advice to senior members of the government on various national security science issues.

Dr. Anastasio received his Ph.D. and M.A. in Theoretical Nuclear Physics from the State University of New York, Stony Brook and a B.A. in Physics, with Honors, from Johns Hopkins University and is a member of Sigma Pi Sigma, National Physics Honor Society. In addition, he has received numerous commendations and is widely recognized for his leadership in national security science and the safe stewardship of nuclear weapons. He is the recipient of the DOE/NNSA Gold Medal, the Distinguished Alumni Award-SUNY Stony Brook, and the DOE Weapons Recognition of Excellence Award for technical leadership in nuclear design.

Bill LaPlante

Dr. William A. LaPlante is Vice President of the Intelligence Portfolio in the National Security Engineering Center, a federally funded research and development center that MITRE operates on behalf of the U.S. Department of Defense. In this role, Dr. LaPlante leads key initiatives in support of the nation's intelligence community.

Dr. LaPlante has more than 30 years of experience in defense technology, most recently as Assistant Secretary of the Air Force for Acquisition. During his three years in that position, Dr. LaPlante led the $43 billion Air Force acquisition enterprise budget, bringing it into alignment with the greater Air Force vision and strategy. Under his leadership, the Air Force reaped nearly $6 billion in "should-cost" savings – the investment of these savings resulted in greater capability for our nation's warfighters. In recognition of his outstanding performance, the Air Force Association awarded Dr. LaPlante the W. Stuart Symington Award for the most significant contribution by a civilian in the field of national defense. In November 2015, the Air Force bestowed on him its Medal for Exceptional Civilian Service, the highest honor it bestows on a civilian employee. And in 2016, the Massachusetts Institute of Technology Security Studies Program presented him with the General James Doolittle Award, in recognition of his contributions to U.S. air power.

Prior to entering public service in 2013, he was MITRE's Missile Defense portfolio director. During this time, Dr. LaPlante was appointed to the Defense Science Board (DSB), where he co-chaired a study on enhancing the adaptability of U.S. military forces. He has resumed his participation in the DSB, where he advises top Department of Defense leadership on critical scientific and technological topics related to the effectiveness of the nation's military forces.

Before joining MITRE, he was the department head for Global Engagement at the Johns Hopkins University Applied Physics Laboratory (APL). In that role he was responsible for all of APL's work supporting offensive military capabilities. He was also a member of the APL Executive Council.

He holds a bachelor's degree in engineering physics from the University of Illinois, a master's degree in applied physics from Johns Hopkins University, and a doctorate in mechanical engineering from Catholic University of America.

DOCUMENTS SUBMITTED FOR THE RECORD

March 9, 2017

Comments on *Peer Review and Design Competition in the NNSA National Security Laboratories**

Roy Schwitters

January 11, 2016

On 1/5/2016, I received an email from the Counsel to the Strategic Forces Subcommittee of the House Armed Services Committee, inviting me to testify the following Tuesday, 1/12/2016 to the Subcommittee to provide context and alternative perspective on a recommendation to build new prototypes of nuclear weapons made in the recent NAS report on peer review and design competition in the NNSA national security laboratories (for reference, see footnote below; in this note, I refer to this document as "the NAS report"). Due to other commitments, I declined the invitation to testify. This note outlines my views on the subject NAS report.

Briefly, the NAS report deals with two crucial issues in stockpile stewardship: 1) providing quality assurance in the maintenance of the nuclear deterrent through inter-laboratory peer review, and 2) developing and retaining technical staff, both under the Nation's moratorium on explosive nuclear testing. In my view, the conclusions and recommendations regarding peer review are generally supportive of policies implemented by NNSA and its national laboratories during 2008-2010, with useful suggestions for extension and improvement. On the other hand, its second major recommendation, to develop new prototype nuclear weapons not to be entered into the stockpile, is so vague and poorly supported that it cannot be analyzed in a serious way. The intent of the recommendation, to provide important, challenging technical problems that will attract and retain qualified scientists and engineers to careers in the stockpile stewardship program, must be part of any long-term strategy to maintain the nation's nuclear deterrence, but the proposal outlined in the NAS report provides no basis for anticipating its value to U.S. deterrence, its chances of success, or its potential for launching unintended deleterious consequences. Finally, the report is spotty in terms of level of detail and is lacking in clarity, which must make it difficult, at best, for anyone not already immersed in details of the U.S. nuclear weapons program to understand what is being proposed.

I what follows, I give a personal synopsis of the report, followed by additional comments.

---

* Report of the Committee on Peer Review and Design Competition Related to Nuclear Weapons, The National Academies Press (2015).

The NAS Report, a Brief Synopsis

The NAS report was the product of a committee organized through the National Academies and chaired by Paul Peercy and Jill Dahlburg. The study commenced in June 2014 and completed with the recent release of the report by NAS in late 2015. The Administrator of the National Nuclear Security Administration commissioned the study in response to Congressional language. The charge followed by the committee was:

> "Assess the following:
>
> - The quality and effectiveness of peer review of designs, development plans, engineering and scientific activities, and priorities related to both nuclear and non-nuclear aspects of nuclear weapons;
> - Incentives for effective peer review;
> - The potential effectiveness, efficiency, and cost of alternative methods of conducting peer review and design competition related to both nuclear and non-nuclear aspects of nuclear weapons, as compared to current methods;
> - Known instances where current peer review practices and design competition succeeded or failed in finding problems or potential problems; and
> - How peer review practices related to both nuclear and non-nuclear aspects of nuclear weapons should be adjusted as the three NNSA laboratories transition to a broader national security mission."

The report lists four basic sets of conclusions with accompanying recommendations. The first set addresses the first two bulleted elements of the charge, concluding that the peer review process is used effectively by all three NNSA laboratories (Los Alamos, Livermore, and Sandia), that incentives for peer review at the laboratories "are abundantly evident", that somewhat different approaches are used by the labs, and that there are opportunities for improvement.

Conclusion/Recommendation Set 2 focuses on aspects of design competition raised by the third bulleted point in the study charge, but falls short of addressing all the questions. The NAS report does not address effectiveness, efficiency, and cost of alternative approaches of either peer review or design competition. The Set 2 recommendation argues for maintaining "independent design capabilities" at Los Alamos and Livermore "to enable independent peer review of critical technical issues", a position I strongly endorse.

Conclusion/Recommendation Set 3 assesses various deficiencies of the RRW design competition process and suggests remedies in peer review processes, which seem to have been largely addressed by the INWAP. This would appear to represent the committee's response to a "failed" design competition/peer review practice.

Conclusion 4 states: "In contrast to the robust state of peer review at the NNSA laboratories, the state of design competition is not robust." Recommendation 4 goes on to assert that a series of design competitions that "exercise the full set of design skills necessary for an effective nuclear deterrent" and *not* contribute designs that would enter the stockpile would attract a workforce to maintain the future viability of the nation's nuclear deterrent.

The last element of the charge—how peer review ... should be adjusted as the three NNSA laboratories transition to a broader national security mission—doesn't appear, at least to me, to be addressed in the four conclusion-recommendation sections.

A Personal Assessment of Certain Aspects of the NAS Report

The crux of the report is contained in Conclusion/Recommendation Set 4. Whether the single word "robust" is sufficient to describe adequately the key issues necessary to maintain the nation's future nuclear deterrent, Conclusion 4 seems to aptly summarize this report: peer review is in pretty good shape and, with some tweaks of the INWAP process (chiefly having Sandia follow peer review procedures that engage Los Alamos and Livermore personnel or a broader range of topics than annual assessment), can work well as long as competent, motivated, and imaginative technical people are committed to the program.

Recommendation 4 focuses only on design competitions. There is no explanation of how such competitions would be formulated or how a winner would be selected. I simply do not understand how such a vague plan to engage design experts can possibly achieve the important objective, to which I subscribe, of maintaining the technical expertise and vitality of NNSA's laboratories—and its unique production capabilities.

Why is the challenge space limited to design? There are many key technical capabilities essential to maintaining the nuclear deterrent. It is a truism that capabilities must be exercised to be maintained—"use it or lose it!" What other capabilities might need regular exercise, not available during normal LEP cycles, for example?

What does one do with the successful/unsuccessful results generated from a competition? Do they cause cost concerns or proliferation concerns that will actually harm stockpile stewardship? After a few cycles in such a campaign of competitions, will the process still satisfy the fundamental need to attract and retain key people?

The report is unclear and can be misinterpreted in important sections. For example, how is a non-expert to understand the statement under Conclusion 1.3 (page 2): "With only archival nuclear explosion test data available, …"? Unmentioned are all the other data that have been and are being actively acquired and analyzed. What is a "NEP laboratory"? Is it true that "peer review … is recognized as a means of ensuring high-quality work products? Does "QMU systematically apply the output of the Stockpile Stewardship Program … to assessment of the stockpile? There are other examples of non-sequiturs inadvertently created in the report, which could lead to misunderstanding of important messages. More careful editing would have been well worth the additional time and effort.

Richard L. Garwin
1 Christie Place Unit 402W
Scarsdale, NY 10583
(914) 945-2555
Email: RLG2@us.ibm.com
URL: www.fas.org/RLG/

January 11, 2016

Chairman Mike Rogers
Ranking Member Jim Cooper
Strategic Forces Subcommittee
House Armed Services Committee
Rayburn 2216
House of Representatives
Washington, DC 20515

Dear Mike Rogers and Jim Cooper,

The NAS report on "Peer Review and Design Competition ..." provides useful commentary on peer review and background on the nuclear weapons design and maintenance process.

However, I believe that the great emphasis on "design competition" in the nature of competitive designs of new warheads for missiles or bombs seriously misses the point and does not assess the very substantial costs-- both opportunity costs and the spur that such a program gives to international competitors and potential enemies, who have much more to gain from innovations and weapon development than does the United States. The appearance of continuous active nuclear weapon design competition can have negative as well as positive benefit.

I particularly take exception to the argument that the U.S. nuclear deterrent is impaired by the lack of a visible series of competitive designs and prototyping of new nuclear warheads and bombs. I can understand that whatever the merit of an argument, it can apparently be strengthened by indicating that without the proposed program, U.S. deterrence of nuclear war or war in general will suffer,

> *"p. 5: they did not exercise the complete set of skills required in the NNSA complex to design nuclear weapons that would be an effective deterrent, nor was the credibility of any design assessed by fabricating a device or by non-nuclear testing."*

but we have had experience with this argument before:

> In support of the National Ignition Facility, in the years following the 1992 moratorium on nuclear testing initiated by the Administration of President George H.W. Bush, it was argued that without continued nuclear explosion testing, evident the world over by seismic records of the underground nuclear explosions at the U.S. national test site, nuclear deterrence could be maintained only by the achievement of "ignition" at NIF. I took the other side in this discussion, arguing that such a proposal was self-serving and

that the argument itself contributed to the *weakening* of deterrence, because the United States clearly had many nuclear weapons which had been tested and could be maintained indefinitely in the future by what is known now as a LEP (Life Extension Program); More particularly, the suggestion that such a force-in-being of tested nuclear weapons suffered in deterrent value because ignition could not be achieved in a charge of fusion fuel a million times smaller than that in a weapon was both logically deficient and both politically and technically wrong headed. Unforeseen difficulties, either in principle or in practice might prevent the achievement of ignition at NIF, without in any way impairing the continued ability of the United States to produce two-stage thermonuclear weapons.

And that is how it turned out—failure to achieve ignition, but few had believed the hype.

Thus I think it is highly undesirable to argue that routine design competitions, through the prototype stage of the nuclear explosive package-- NEP-- are essential to the maintenance of robust U.S. nuclear deterrence.

In fact, I have no animosity to the idea of design competition and proposed such in a paper of 2008 and in my testimony to the congressionally mandated Commission on the Strategic Posture of the United States.[1] As for motivation of the technical teams in the two NNSA design labs, I judge that effectively contributing to the continuing effectiveness of the stockpile through life extension programs (LEP) is judged a worthier goal than winning a football-game-like competition.

There are very substantial costs associated with such design competition, and goals of infrastructure advancement should be to reduce greatly the cost of activities in the U.S. nuclear weapon design laboratories, and also the time required for planning, programming, and carrying out such programs.

Furthermore, the Report states, *"Moreover, as other nations pursue new designs or strategies that could constitute serious threat evolutions, the United States could find itself in a precarious security situation were it not to maintain nuclear weapon design, development, and production skills to address such evolving demands. "* implying that new U.S. nuclear weapons would be necessary to respond to new nuclear weapon designs by others. This is rarely the case.

The Report makes a stab at stating the magnitude of the effort required in such a design competition,

> *"Roughly speaking, the committee imagines a design competition as involving a few dozen laboratory staff members, with a larger number in the first year of each competition, plus some prototype development and experiments up to and including hydrodynamic tests. These parameters suggest a scale for the endeavor that the committee deems appropriate."*

---

[1] http://fas.org/rlg/9007TEST1.pdf

https://www.armscontrol.org/act/2008_12/Garwin "A Different Kind of Complex: The Future of U.S. Nuclear Weapons and the Nuclear Weapons Enterprise," by R.L. Garwin includes

"Yet, the work done so far on the RRW program has re-energized the nuclear laboratories and their involvement in the nuclear weapons complex. Such a major effort should be undertaken every five years or so. I know firsthand from my involvement with this program that new insights have arisen from the new focus on simulation and computation."

but the authors neither provide any rationale for this statement, nor work out its program cost or opportunity cost. And in my opinion it does not go far enough, because the NEP is not a weapon in itself, until it is integrated with the bomb or warhead, on which it puts demands, and which, in turn, influence the design of the NEP.

The load and vibration characteristics of Navy and Air Force-strategic reentry vehicles and their corresponding NEPs are quite different-- posing now well-recognized impediments to the "3 + 2" approach.

The Labs do important work in areas of nonproliferation and counter-terrorism, in a much larger volume of design space than would be involved in analyzing and developing alternative warheads for the U.S. stockpile. As with learning a foreign language, this provides insights into elements of U.S. weapons.

Since the Administration of President George H.W. Bush, the U.S. nuclear weapon program has been based on the judgment that the U.S. does not need new nuclear weapon capabilities-- a judgment that I share. The continued viability of the nuclear deterrent has been focused on ensuring that the U.S. nuclear weapons will continue to function decade after decade, by LEPs that include, if necessary, production of new plutonium pits, refreshment of the high explosive and other elements subject to deterioration, and the substitution of thoroughly tested components either in the NEP or external to it.

It should be repeated that many of the aspects of a nuclear explosion important in wartime have never been tested in underground nuclear explosion tests, where the NEP is at rest, surrounded by rock rather than by air, not subject to rotation or deceleration in the range of tens of times that of gravity, and the like. It is strange, therefore, that the essential role of realistic "flight testing" now achieved with the "HFJTA"—High-Fidelity Joint Test Assembly-- is eliminated from the requirement for prototypes.

Finally, if the United States argues that the continued development and readiness for manufacture of nuclear weapons with new characteristics is essential to its deterrence, how can other states resist such arguments from their nuclear weapon establishments? Is it really in the United States interest to have vigorous competitions not only between two U.S. nuclear weapon design laboratories but also among all the weapon labs of the world? And what impact will ongoing vigorous design competitions have on the resolve of non-nuclear-weapon state members of the NPT to support the NPT and the CTBT?

Far better is continued emphasis on improving the robustness of command and control, surety of nuclear weapons storage and transport, and increased capability for preventing nuclear weapon theft.
    / Richard L. Garwin /

Richard L. Garwin
Relevant biography at https://www.armscontrol.org/act/2008_12/Garwin and also appended.

Richard L. Garwin was born in Cleveland, Ohio, in 1928. He received the B.S. in Physics from Case Institute of Technology, Cleveland, in 1947, and the Ph.D. in Physics from the University of Chicago in 1949.

He is IBM Fellow Emeritus at the Thomas J. Watson Research Center, Yorktown Heights, New York. After three years on the faculty of the University of Chicago, he joined IBM Corporation in 1952, and was until June 1993 IBM Fellow at the Thomas J. Watson Research Center, Yorktown Heights, New York. In addition, he is a consultant to the U.S. government on matters of military technology, arms control, etc. He has been Director of the IBM Watson Laboratory, Director of Applied Research at the IBM Thomas J. Watson Research Center, a member of the IBM Corporate Technical Committee, Adjunct Research Fellow in the Kennedy School of Government, Harvard University; and Adjunct Professor of Physics at Columbia University. He has also been Professor of Public Policy in the Kennedy School of Government, Harvard University. From 1997 to 2004 he was Philip D. Reed Senior Fellow for Science and Technology at the Council on Foreign Relations, New York.

He has made contributions in the design of nuclear weapons, in instruments and electronics for research in nuclear and low-temperature physics, in the establishment of the nonconservation of parity and the demonstration of some of its striking consequences, in computer elements and systems, including superconducting devices, in communication systems, in the behavior of solid helium, in the detection of gravitational radiation, and in military technology. He has published more than 500 papers and been granted 47 U.S. patents. He has testified to many Congressional committees on matters involving national security, transportation, energy policy and technology, and the like. He is coauthor of many books, among them Nuclear Weapons and World Politics (1977), Nuclear Power Issues and Choices (1977), Energy: The Next Twenty Years (1979), Science Advice to the President (1980), Managing the Plutonium Surplus: Applications and Technical Options (1994), Feux Follets et Champignons Nucleaires (1997) (in French with Georges Charpak), Megawatts and Megatons: A Turning Point in the Nuclear Age? (2001) (with Georges Charpak), and "De Tchernobyl en tchernobyls," (with Georges Charpak and Venance Journe) (2005).

He was a member of the President's Science Advisory Committee 1962-65 and 1969-72, and of the Defense Science Board 1966-69. He is a Fellow of the American Physical Society, of the IEEE, and of the American Academy of Arts and Sciences; and a member of the National Academy of Sciences, the Institute of Medicine, the National Academy of Engineering, the Council on Foreign Relations, and the American Philosophical Society. He served on the Council of the National Academy of Sciences 1983-1986 and 2002-2005.

The citation accompanying his 1978 election to the U.S. National Academy of Engineering reads "Contributions applying the latest scientific discoveries to innovative practical engineering applications contributing to national security and economic growth." He received the 1983 Wright Prize for interdisciplinary scientific achievement, the 1988 AAAS Scientific Freedom and Responsibility Award, the 1991 Erice "Science for Peace" Prize, from the U.S. Government the 1996 R.V. Jones Foreign Intelligence Award and the 1996 Enrico Fermi Award, the Federation of American Scientists: Public Service Award 1971 and 1997, University of Chicago Enrico Fermi Institute and Departments of Physics and Astronomy: Public Service Medal (2002), Case Alumni Association: Gold Medal (2002), Academie des Sciences (France): La Grande Medaille de l'Academie des Sciences-2002, and Fellow of the IEEE (November 2003) "for contributions to the application of engineering to national defense." In 2003 he received from the President the National Medal of Science.

From 1977 to 1985 he was on the Council of the Institute for Strategic Studies (London), and during 1978 he chaired the Panel on Public Affairs of the American Physical Society. He is a long-time member of Pugwash and has served on the Pugwash Council.

His work for the government has included studies on antisubmarine warfare, new technologies in health care, sensor systems, military and civil aircraft, and satellite and strategic systems, from the point of view of improving such systems as well as assessing existing capabilities. For example, he contributed to the first U.S. photographic reconnaissance satellite program, CORONA, that returned 3 million feet of film from more than 100 successful flights 1960-1972. He contributed also to the current electro-optical imaging systems and various electronic intelligence satellite systems deployed by the U.S. government.

He has been a member of the Scientific Advisory Group to the Joint Strategic Target Planning Staff and was in 1998 a Commissioner on the 9-person "Rumsfeld" Commission to Assess the Ballistic Missile Threat to the United States. From 1993 to August 2001, he chaired the Arms Control and Nonproliferation Advisory Board of the Department of State. On the 40th anniversary of the founding of the National Reconnaissance Office (NRO) he was recognized as one of the ten Founders of National Reconnaissance.

Since 2009 he has been a consultant to the Office of Science and Technology Policy in the Executive Offices of the President. In 2010 he was a consultant to Secretary of Energy Steve Chu on the Deep Water Horizon (BP) oil spill, and in 2011 he supported Secretary Chu again on the U.S. response to the damaged reactors at Fukushima Dai-ichi.

(Biography current as of 08/13/12)

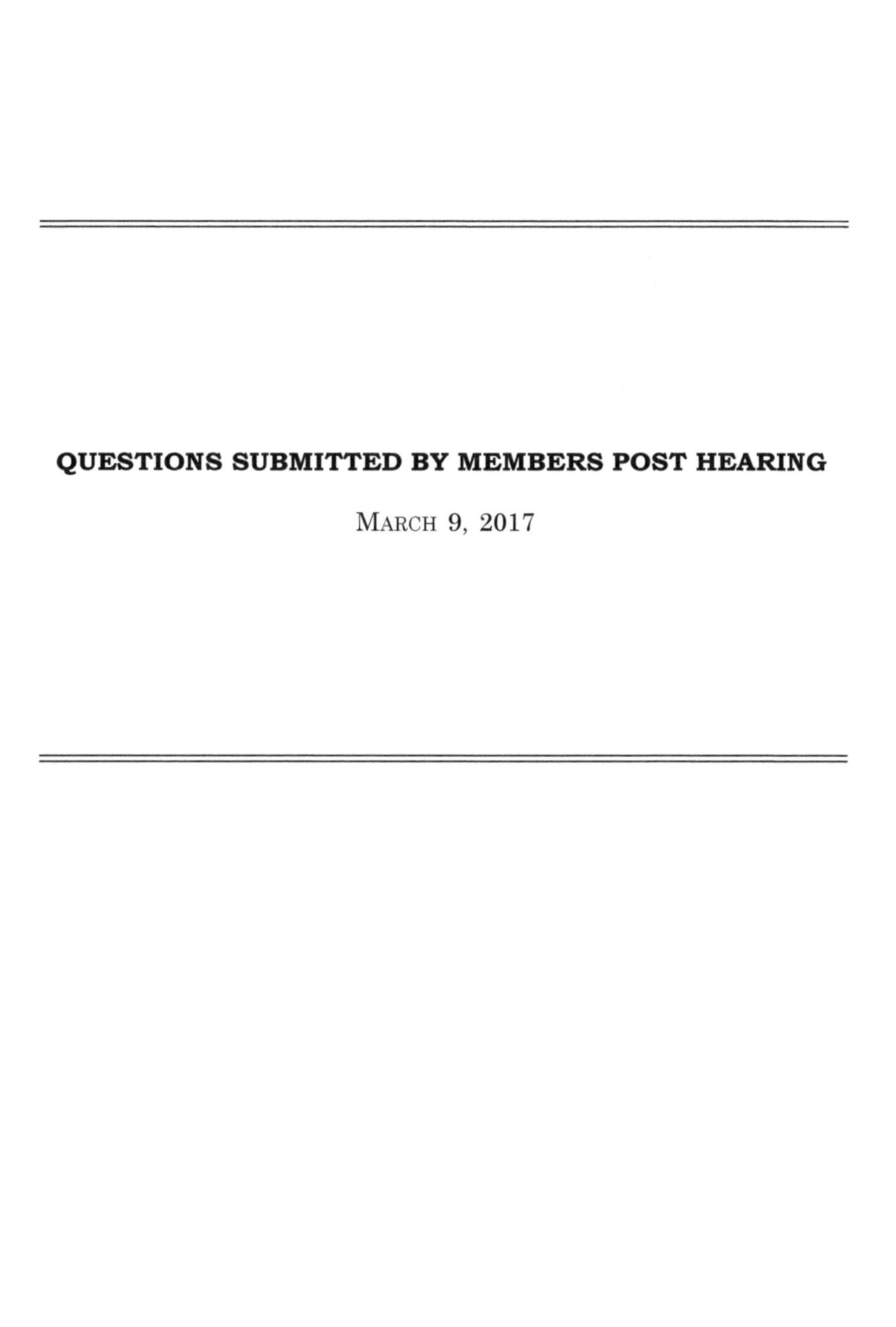

QUESTIONS SUBMITTED BY MEMBERS POST HEARING

MARCH 9, 2017

QUESTIONS SUBMITTED BY MR. ROGERS

Mr. ROGERS. What are your recommendations regarding how the Stockpile Responsiveness Program authorized by Congress in the FY16 NDAA, and the foreign design prototyping requirement in the FY15 NDAA, could be improved to better tackle the concerns expressed by the DSB? What actions should the administration take here? What actions should Congress take here?

Dr. JOHN, Dr. ANASTASIO, and Dr. LAPLANTE. As stated in the "Seven Defense Priorities..." report, the DSB believes that a hedge against uncertainty is as important a part of the nation's nuclear weapons program as both the certification of the current systems and the life extension or replacement of systems that have aged out. The foreign design prototyping requirement, known as the Foreign Nuclear Weapons Initiative (FNWI) in the FY15 NDAA and the Stockpile Responsiveness Program in the FY16 NDAA were positive steps to support such hedging, but their focus is on DOE. Two ways the Stockpile Responsiveness Program could be more effective would be through the participation of the DOD and with Congressional funding of the Program, to include options for prototyping promising concepts. The FNWI would also benefit from a DOD partnership to posit a set of signatures not just of threat warheads, but also system and operational capabilities for which the intelligence community could monitor as early as possible.

Mr. ROGERS. Please describe why the DSB thinks it is important to truly flex all of the muscles needed to build nuclear weapons from scratch? Why don't life extension programs flex all of these muscles?

Dr. JOHN, Dr. ANASTASIO, and Dr. LAPLANTE. The DSB has confidence in the current U.S. stockpile but believes that the nuclear weapons have aged well beyond their expected lifetimes with no margin to further extend their life. Life extension programs (LEPs) for existing delivery platforms and warheads are essential to sustain the safety, security, and reliability of our currently fielded systems, but only go so far and do not produce a fully modernized system with a long life, nor do they address the growing concerns about our ability to be flexible in the face of unpredictable threats. However, LEPs are replacement programs that rebuild fashion, legacy system which originated during the last decades of the Cold War. They do not exercise the full scope of activities across the spectrum of concept development, design, engineering, production, and certification. To be sure, LEPs often involve some level of component or subsystem redesign and certification as duplicate replacement parts may no longer be available. But they do not start from a "clean sheet" for the entire system in which the options that would optimize the system for the purposes the nation might need can be explored—whether that optimization be fore performance, improved margin, employment of new manufacturing techniques, etc. The DSB recognized this shortcoming in an LEP approach as early as 2004 and again in 2006, as limiting flexibility against an uncertain future, and calling for research to meet emerging needs for east of manufacture, higher margins, lower collateral damage, and special effects. If the nation ever decided it needed something different, the DOD–DOE partnership would need to recreate skills that have atrophied over the last 25 years in the context of different requirements and constraints (such as modern delivery platforms or no nuclear testing).

Mr. ROGERS. The DSB report indicates that U.S. nuclear force planning must do a better job anticipating threats and be ready to respond to them. What are some of those threats? How should our nuclear forces programs and enterprise be postured to respond to them? Do DOD, NNSA, and the IC have an active and ongoing effort to anticipate threats in the nuclear weapons realm? What is it? What can Congress do to help ensure DOD and NNSA are effectively and actively working to anticipate threats?

Dr. JOHN, Dr. ANASTASIO, and Dr. LAPLANTE. [A classified response was provided and is retained in committee files.]

Mr. ROGERS. The DSB's report from December emphasizes that "nuclear weapons are a steadily evolving threat." Would you please describe how the nuclear weapons threat has evolved, particularly since the last Nuclear Posture Review (NPR) was written in 2010? What new threats, vulnerability, or opportunities have emerged or changed since 2010 that the new NPR must take a clear-eyed look at?

(51)

Dr. JOHN, Dr. ANASTASIO, and Dr. LAPLANTE. Since the late 1990s, Russia has been on a path to emphasize nuclear weapons as an integral part of its security strategy by modernizing its strategic forces, expanding its tactical capabilities, and promulgating and exercising new doctrine for regional and strategic use. Since the 2010 Nuclear Posture Review, the breakdown of any further U.S.-Russia arms control discussions, Russian violation of the Intermediate Range Nuclear Forces treaty, and its aggressive actions along its borders have occurred. Russia's threatening actions on the borders with U.S. NATO partners raised concerns about the alliance's commitment to mutual defense. In addition, China made nuclear modernization and expansion of its strategic arsenal a key part of its massive military expansion and continued to surprise the U.S. with the speed at which it has fielded new systems. North Korea has continued to develop and operationalize its own nuclear force seemingly without more price to pay than it already has. In both technical and operational aspects, Russia and China are introducing asymmetries in nuclear capabilities and concepts of operation that incorporates nuclear warfighting options in a more integrated—or "cross-domain"—approach with non-nuclear forces. North Korea's opacity creates numerous questions as to what capabilities would best deter it from further proliferation or use, and as a result, raises serious concerns in the minds of U.S. regional allies as to whether their interests are better served by having their own nuclear capabilities instead of relying on our extended deterrence guarantees. Depending on how these three situations unfold and how the U.S. addresses them, the potential for further proliferation is serious. Iran has demonstrated the difficult and tenuous nature of stemming a state actor who sees nuclear weapons as a deterrent or hedge against regional threats and as an equalizer against superior non-nuclear military forces. A.Q. Khan, the Pakistani nuclear physicist, demonstrated the ability, even before the advent of such enablers as the dark web, to create an undetected network of nuclear commerce. To complicate matters further, technology is advancing in directions with the potential to make acquisition of a weapon more accessible to those with limited resources.

Mr. ROGERS. What action could the administration or Congress take to improve the readiness and responsiveness of the NNSA enterprise to produce nuclear weapons? Right now, it takes over 15 years to even life extend an existing nuclear weapon—this is far too long. What can we do to drive down timelines while maintaining safety and security (and minimizing costs)?

Dr. JOHN, Dr. ANASTASIO, and Dr. LAPLANTE. The sluggishness of the NNSA enterprise has been recognized as a serious problem through numerous studies, commissions and reviews over two decades, including the 2014 Augustine-Mies Congressional Advisory Panel "A New Foundation for the Nuclear Enterprise." The DSB contribution to this topic came in a 2006 study "Nuclear Capabilities." The DSB observations and recommendations differed little from the other studies both before and after its publication, except that it included both DOE and DOD in its review with the conclusion at that time that "the production complex was not configured, managed, or funded to meet minimum immediate stockpile sustainment needs and that the organization, management, and programs at both DOD and DOE did not provide for a nuclear weapons enterprise capable of meeting the nation's future needs." Leveraging the Stockpile Responsiveness Program to explore design approaches that emphasize readiness and responsiveness provides another avenue to drive down timelines while maintaining safety and security. The governance structure and practices that have burdened the enterprise with excessive oversight, inefficiencies, and mistrust are consistently cited in almost all the dozens of studies as the root problems with NNSA. It remains to be seen whether the Panel to Track and Assess Governance and Management Reform in the Nuclear Security Enterprise, jointly established by the National Academies of Sciences, Engineering, and Medicine and the National Academy of Public Administration at Congressional direction to carry out a 4.5 year assessment of the NNSA's responses to longstanding problems, will provide the forcing function needed to affect the cultural change required to address the inherent problems.

Mr. ROGERS. The DSB report says "The recent uptick in priority for nuclear force modernization in both departments sends a strong message of U.S. commitment to the deterrent, but it comes after 25 years of downplaying (and poorly resourcing) the mission." Would you please describe how this message has resonated within the DOD and NNSA enterprises? Has it improved morale, recruitment, or retention? When the DSB says the mission was poorly resourced, do you believe the nuclear modernization and budget plans laid out now are sufficient?

Dr. JOHN, Dr. ANASTASIO, and Dr. LAPLANTE. The DSB took a detailed look at nuclear skills across both DOD and Doe in 2008 (an expanded version of the 1999 Chiles Commission, also led by ADM Chiles) and identified some serious skills shortfalls fueled by strategy and leadership shortcomings in defining the nature and scope of the nation's nuclear deterrent. In addition, the DSB Permanent Task Force on Nuclear Weapons Surety undertook a series of studies from 2008–2013 focuses on the Air Force in the wake of the accidental transport of a live round from Minot to Barksdale in 2007. Continuing missteps by the Air Force and more recent ones by the Navy led then-Secretary Hagel to request the "Independent Review of the Nuclear Enterprise." The persistent message through these reviews were that the root cause for the operational mishaps linked to airmen and sailor perceptions that the mission was not valued by leadership, as evidenced through their actions that placed greater emphasis on compliance and inspections, and their lack of commitment to address long standing operational support shortfalls. Individual DSB members and a recent study on WMD deterrence are observing that the uptick in priority for nuclear force modernization has definitely improved morale, although there is concern whether this priority will be sustained. The last three Chiefs of Naval Operations have made clear that its nuclear mission is its highest priority. As a result, the Navy has been able to sustain a capable acquisition community and operational force. The Air Force has been slower to change. It is recovering its skill base through a combination of leadership and organizational changes, and is closing funding gaps, but it will require years of sustained support to recreate the spectrum of nuclear skilled military and civilians required. The NNSA laboratories have been growing to meet the demands of the Lifetime Extension Program schedule, with excellent success in attracting highly talented new staff, but they are inexperienced and reliant on a dwindling cadre of experienced (and retirement eligible) scientists and engineers. Sustainment of the current priority placed on the mission, through both words and actions, is the best bet for ensuring retention. The DSB does not comment on specific levels of funding. However, we note that there no funds for DOE/NNSA for plutonium pit production beyond 30 pits/year or for a Stockpile Sustainment Program. For delivery systems, we note that all three legs of the Triad (SSBNs, ICBMs, and bombers) are at the end of their already extended life and will need to be replaced over the next decade and a half. The significant resourcing required will be competing against other priorities in the Department.

Mr. ROGERS. How do we guard against "technology surprise" or "strategic surprise" in the nuclear deterrence realm? Are we putting enough effort into cutting-edge R&D in nuclear capabilities to understand what is possible, what other nations may achieve? Are we putting enough resources into collecting and understanding technical intelligence on other nuclear powers and what capabilities they are researching? What role does prototyping and basic, fundamental nuclear science play here?

Dr. JOHN, Dr. ANASTASIO, and Dr. LaPLANTE. [A classified response was provided and is retained in committee files.]

Mr. ROGERS. The December DSB report says that "Despite the 'peace dividend' at the end of the Cold War, the DSB remains unconvinced that downplaying the nation's nuclear deterrent would lead other nations to do the same." Would you please elaborate on how the DSB believes the U.S. has been downplaying its nuclear deterrent? What actions or policies would you point towards? Have the steps the U.S. has taken to de-emphasize its nuclear deterrent had any effects on the nuclear programs of Russia? China? Any other nuclear power or aspiring nuclear power?

Dr. JOHN, Dr. ANASTASIO, and Dr. LaPLANTE. Successive administrations since the end of the Cold War sought to place more reliance on advanced non-nuclear force capabilities for deterrence while downsizing the nuclear component and focusing investments in that community on life extensions of systems fielded in the 1980s. That strategy, however, had the unintended consequence that nuclear became even more prominent for other nations because they could not afford to meet or overmatch the U.S. with conventional capabilities. Russia began undertaking and extensive modernization and expansion program over a decade earlier than the U.S., China embarked on a steady march to expand both its nuclear and non-nuclear forces, and North Korea became fully committed to developing its own systems irrespective of external pressures. At the same time, the end-of-life of all U.S. systems was known but not addressed until left with no choice, and therefore few options except replacement could be supported in the time remaining. The relatively recent consensus reached by both Congress and the last administration to support the full suite of modernization efforts at both DOD and DOE is a welcome reversal, but any faltering in that commitment going forward will lead to gaps in the viability of the deterrent.

Mr. ROGERS. The DSB's December report makes a pointed summary statement, saying: "In short, 'nuclear' still matters, nuclear is in a class of its own, and nuclear cannot be wished away." What recent actions would you describe as "wishing away" the nuclear aspects of defense? What actions do you think we could take that would again be wishing it away? Or to put it another way—what actions could we take

that would be putting our heads in the sand? Would cancelling key nuclear modernization programs fall in that list?

Dr. JOHN, Dr. ANASTASIO, and Dr. LaPLANTE. [A classified response was provided
and is retained in committee files.]

Mr. ROGERS. Our O&I Subcommittee had a hearing focused on the huge backlog
of deferred maintenance at NNSA's facilities. Has the DSB looked at this issue?
What are the impacts of all of this very old, very decrepit infrastructure? How does
it influence NNSA's readiness and responsiveness to react to new taskings and
changes in programs?

Dr. JOHN and Dr. ANASTASIO. In its "Nuclear Capabilities" report of 2006, the
DSB reported that the production complex was not configured, managed, or funded
to meet minimum immediate stockpile sustainment needs. Many of the problems
that prompted that observation remain, but the DSB has not taken a look at the
issue recently. A glimpse of the advantages that a modern facility employing advanced manufacturing capabilities can provide can be found at the new Kansas City
plant, where non-nuclear components for the weapons are produced.

Mr. ROGERS. What are the key drivers of the U.S. nuclear modernization program? How is it affected by foreign threats and capabilities? How is it affected by
vulnerabilities or aging in current U.S. nuclear forces? Is there margin to further
slip or delay the schedules for our nuclear modernization programs?

Dr. JOHN, Dr. ANASTASIO, and Dr. LaPLANTE. [A classified response was provided
and is retained in committee files.]

Mr. ROGERS. What could be done by DOD—and more broadly DOE and the nation—to "reestablish the knowledge base in nuclear matters and the art of deterrence among both civilian and military leadership," which the DSB notes "has largely atrophied"? What role can Congress play in this?

Dr. JOHN, Dr. ANASTASIO, and Dr. LaPLANTE. The DSB has been consistent
through most of its work on nuclear matters to point out that the most important
part of the nation's deterrent posture is the professional workforce, be they in the
policy, technical, programmatic or operational roles. In no other area of national security do these several dimensions interact as intimately as they do for nuclear matters, such that developing the knowledge and experience to made wise decisions and
take appropriate actions simply takes time. That said, there are some practical
things to be done such as re-introducing the fundamentals of nuclear weapons and
warfighting in the education, training, and exercising activities of the DOD; creating
and promoting promising career paths for military and civilians; and rotating high-
potential professionals through a range of assignments that would expose them to
the policy, technical, and operational considerations associated with nuclear deterrence. In addition, respectful debate about the merits of various contributors to deterrence should be encouraged. Contrary to the current perception held by many,
the U.S. deterrence posture of the Cold War was constantly evolving as the country
tested and implemented ideas, keeping some and discarding others, and as non-nuclear capabilities advanced. In the more complex 21st century multi-polar environment, the U.S. is at the beginning of developing new strategies for deterrence and
should expect those strategies to evolve as we get smarter about the threats it faces.

Mr. ROGERS. Please describe the DSB's concerns on whether DOD's conventional
forces are adequately prepared to "fight through" a nuclear environment. What
should DOD be doing to ensure nuclear survivability requirements are included in
key DOD acquisition programs? How should DOD examine tactics, redundancy, and
recovery plans to ensure it can "fight through"?

Dr. JOHN, Dr. ANASTASIO, and Dr. LaPLANTE. [A classified response was provided
and is retained in committee files.]

Mr. ROGERS. Please talk us through the following recommendation the DSB made:
"The DSB strongly recommends that all major acquisitions be born with a nuclear
survivability requirement derived from projected threat scenarios relevant to the
range of missions expected for the system." DOD doesn't already do this? Which
major DOD acquisition programs are subject to nuclear hardening requirements—
or requirements to be able to "fight through"—and which are not?

Dr. JOHN, Dr. ANASTASIO, and Dr. LaPLANTE. [A classified response was provided
and is retained in committee files.]

Mr. ROGERS. What is the state of knowledge and expertise in DOD and the defense industry regarding nuclear weapons effects and survivability? What could be
done to improve this knowledge level? What steps should Congress take here?

Dr. JOHN, Dr. ANASTASIO, and Dr. LaPLANTE. Through its work in the area of nuclear weapons effects and survivability over the decade from 2005–2015, the DSB
observed that expertise was initially continuing to decline as it had since the end
of the Cold War. The area started to draw attention, however, because of a number
of activities, such as the EMP Commission and the follow-on DSB Work through the

standing committee, the B61–12 program, and leadership at the Defense Threat Reduction Agency (DTRA). While those coincident efforts did not result in restoration of Cold War levels of investment or expertise, they did stem the decline and produced a more stable programmatic situation at DTRA and the National Nuclear Security Agency (NNSA) laboratories. That stabilization and even modest growth has persisted as a result of the triad related modernization programs. In the past ~three years, there have also been investments in applying the computational and above-ground simulator tools of NNSA's Stockpile Stewardship Program to advancing the science of weapons effects. The DSB has observed, however, that this area has been a relatively poor sibling to the weapons physics community. We recommended a more effective "national" enterprise in which DTRA and the NNSA laboratories were seamlessly partnered. Such a partnership could create a more viable capability to better serve the needs of both Departments and the defense industry which has largely lost its in-house design, development, and testing expertise.

Mr. ROGERS. Please describe the history of the DSB's work on nuclear deterrence issues. How long has DSB been working in this topic? What are the backgrounds and expertise of the DSB members who contribute to its work on nuclear deterrence?

Dr. JOHN. The DSB has worked on nuclear issues since its inception 60 years ago. The list below covers work since 2004.

- Nuclear in the Context of Broader Themes—Defense Imperatives for a New Administration, 2008
- Capability Surprise (2008 Summer Study), 2009
- Strategic Surprise (2014 Summer Study), 2015
- Deterring, Preventing, and Responding to the Threat or Use of WMD, 2017 (in review)
- Nuclear Technologies and Systems—Future Strategic Strike Forces (2003 Summer Study), 2004
- Employment of the National Ignition Facility (NIF), 2004
- Future Strategic Strike Skills, 2006
- Technology and Innovation Enablers for Superiority in 2030 (2012 Summer Study), 2013
- Assessment of Nuclear Monitoring and Verification Technologies, 2014
- Operations (Reports of the Permanent Task Force on Nuclear Weapons Surety) Report on the Unauthorized Movement of Nuclear Weapons, 2008
- Nuclear Weapons Inspections for the Strategic Nuclear Force, 2008
- Independent Assessment of the Air Force Nuclear Enterprise, 2011
- Air Force Nuclear Enterprise Follow-On Review, 2013
- Nuclear Survivability and Weapons Effects Nuclear Weapons Effects Test, Evaluation, and Simulation, 2005
- Nuclear Weapons Effects National Enterprise, 2010
- Reports of the Standing Task Force on Survivability of DOD Systems and Assets to Electromagnetic Pulse (EMP) and other Nuclear Weapon Effects, #1–5, 2011–2015
- Unconventional Nuclear Strike Preventing and Defending Against Clandestine Nuclear Attack, 2004
- Reducing Vulnerabilities to Weapons of Mass Desctruction (2005 Summer Study), 2007
- Skills and the Health of the Enterprise Nuclear Capabilities, 2006
- Nuclear Deterrence Skills, 2008

Each report lists the members of the task force. While not replicating that here, the participants have included retired senior civilians and general/flag officers who made their careers in DOD's nuclear weapons community, with backgrounds that span the policy, technical, acquisition, and operational areas. Positions held include former STRATCOM commanders, Air Force Chiefs, Navy submarine force and nuclear weapons systems program leaders, Assistant Secretaries of Defense from OSD (Policy) and OSD (AT&L), and technical leadership from the Defense Threat Reduction Agency and the Intelligence Community. Participants were also drawn from senior leadership of DOD's Federally Funded Research and Development Centers (FFRDCs) and the Energy Department's nuclear weapons laboratories, and form industries involved in both the platform and technical services aspects related to nuclear weapons. To keep entrenched perspectives in check, most studies also include task force members whose expertise is in related fields (e.g., cyber ISR, missile defense) but not mainstream nuclear matters.

QUESTIONS SUBMITTED BY MR. COOPER

Mr. COOPER. The report suggests the potential need to return to nuclear testing, noting that: "Underground nuclear testing provided both stockpile confidence and a powerful tool in advancing scientific understanding, but nuclear testing has not been permitted ... In its place, the nation supported the Stockpile Stewardship Program that significantly improved the fundamental understanding of material aging and nuclear explosive physics through above ground simulators, and state-of-the-art computational modeling. An open question remains as to how long one can have confidence in the weapons through these approaches alone." (emphasis added).

While recognizing that the Board did not consider policy implications or cost considerations, please explain whether and how the report recommends reconsidering the need for nuclear testing? [Question #46, for cross-reference.]

Dr. JOHN and Dr. ANASTASIO. Nuclear testing was one of several tools used to develop the U.S. stockpile and advance scientific understanding during the Cold War. With the end of the Cold War the nation put in place the Stockpile Stewardship Program that has been remarkably successful in providing the technical basis for continued sufficient confidence in the current stockpile. As part of the DSB's highlighting the need for a hedge to an uncertain future, we have raised the question of how long this approach alone will provide the needed confidence. The DSB has not made a recommendation of how and/or when the need for nuclear testing should be reconsidered, but note that there is an existing process of annual assessment by the Commander U.S. Strategic Command and each of the national security laboratory directors regarding the need to return to nuclear testing.

Mr. COOPER. Is nuclear deterrence just about U.S. nuclear forces? What else contributes to deterrence? [Question #47, for cross-reference.]

Dr. JOHN and Dr. ANASTASIO. While the Triad represents the most visible manifestation of deterrence and is overdue for modernization, there are many other factors that contribute to deterrence and also require attention. Together with the Triad, these factors present to any adversary the credibility that the U.S. is fully capable of executing against our strategy under any circumstance; namely that the U.S. can impose unacceptable costs and/or negate any perceived benefits of an adversary's actions. They include: The operational readiness of the force as demonstrated through training and exercises; The ability and capacity of the technical enterprise to anticipate and respond to changes in the threat; The ability to operate in an adversary generated nuclear environment (referred to as nuclear survivability); A robust command and control system; Preventing further proliferation—both "vertically" by current nuclear weapons actors, and "horizontally" by new proliferators—through the tools of diplomacy (treaties and agreements), cooperative and unilateral monitoring, and assurance/extended deterrence to our allies. The lynchpin: the demonstrated skills of talented, knowledgeable, committed, and valued people. The DSB has addressed each of these areas (with the exception of command and control, a topic covered by special commissions and the subject of a new DSB study just getting underway) in some depth throughout its history, and especially over the past 15 years as we began to see worrisome trends in the threat. A relatively recent proposition to add to the above list is that integration of U.S. advanced non-nuclear capabilities with its nuclear forces—so-called cross-domain, or integrated, deterrence—holds promise as a more fulsome approach. Over the last three decades the U.S. has developed highly effective non-nuclear capabilities to hold targets at risk that only nuclear weapons could previously. Several of these capabilities—kinetic and non-kinetic—seem likely to be able to enhance the credibility of both the nuclear deterrent and the extended deterrent if effectively employed as part of a broader integrated deterrence strategy. Each of the capabilities have the potential to affect the confidence the adversary can hold in his offensive nuclear capability to achieve a military or diplomatic purpose. These non-nuclear capabilities include the application of the technologies of autonomy, precision conventional strike, and space and cyber operations. Successful integration will require a seamless command and control system across nuclear and non-nuclear warfighting domains.

Mr. COOPER. The DSB report recommends developing weapons with lower yields. What is the need or benefit when we already have non-strategic nuclear weapons that have low yields?

Dr. JOHN and Dr. ANASTASIO. The DSB did not recommend the development of nuclear weapons with lower yields. We did state that the U.S. should have a robust hedge against an uncertain future and that one consideration for such a hedge could be low yield options for existing weapons beside the B61.

Mr. COOPER. How have advances in technologies made it easier for aspiring nuclear weapons states or even terrorists to acquire nuclear weapons? What investments should we make to keep ahead of this threat?

Dr. JOHN and Dr. ANASTASIO. [A classified response was provided and is retained in committee files.]

Mr. COOPER. What could be done by DOD—and more broadly DOE—to "reestablish the knowledge base in nuclear matters and the art of deterrence among both civilian and military leadership," which the DSB notes "has largely atrophied"? What role can Congress play in supporting this effort?

Dr. JOHN and Dr. ANASTASIO. The DSB has been consistent through most of its work on nuclear matters to point out that the most important part of the nation's deterrent posture is the professional workforce, be they in the policy, technical, programmatic or operational roles. In no other area of national security do these several dimensions interact as intimately as they do for nuclear matters, such that developing the knowledge and experience to made wise decisions and take appropriate actions simply takes time. That said, there are some practical things to be done such as re-introducing the fundamentals of nuclear weapons and warfighting in the education, training, and exercising activities of the DOD; creating and promoting promising career paths for military and civilians; and rotating high-potential professionals through a range of assignments that would expose them to the policy, technical, and operational considerations associated with nuclear deterrence. In addition, respectful debate about the merits of various contributors to deterrence should be encouraged. Contrary to the current perception held by many, the U.S. deterrence posture of the Cold War was constantly evolving as the country tested and implemented ideas, keeping some and discarding others, and as non-nuclear capabilities advanced. In the more complex 21st century multi-polar environment, the U.S. is at the beginning of developing new strategies for deterrence and should expect those strategies to evolve as we get smarter about the threats it faces.

QUESTIONS SUBMITTED BY MR. FRANKS

Mr. FRANKS. The DSB reports that "nuclear testing has not been permitted for 25 years" and "an open question remains as to how long one can have confidence in the weapons" by pursuing the Stockpile Stewardship Program but no full-scale nuclear testing.

Does it believe our science-based tools will be enough to certify the reliability of the stockpile for the long term or may we need to return to nuclear testing at some point?

Dr. JOHN, Dr. ANASTASIO, and Dr. LaPLANTE. As part the DSB's highlighting the need for a hedge to an uncertain future we have raised the question of how long this approach alone will provide the needed confidence. (See also the answer to question 46.) [Question #46 can be found on page 56.]

Mr. FRANKS. What could be done by DOD, DOE, and Congress to "reestablish the knowledge base in nuclear matters and the art of deterrence among both civilian and military leadership," which the DSB notes "has largely atrophied"? What are we doing to ensure our nuclear scientists and engineers are able to design and build new nuclear warheads if they were called upon to do so?

Dr. JOHN, Dr. ANASTASIO, and Dr. LaPLANTE. The DSB has been consistent through most of its work on nuclear matters to point out that the most important part of the nation's deterrent posture is the professional workforce, be they in the policy, technical, programmatic or operational roles. In no other area of national security do these several dimensions interact as intimately as they do for nuclear matters, such that developing the knowledge and experience to made wise decisions and take appropriate actions simply takes time. That said, there are some practical things to be done such as re-introducing the fundamentals of nuclear weapons and warfighting in the education, training, and exercising activities of the DOD; creating and promoting promising career paths for military and civilians; and rotating high-potential professionals through a range of assignments that would expose them to the policy, technical, and operational considerations associated with nuclear deterrence. In addition, respectful debate about the merits of various contributors to deterrence should be encouraged. Contrary to the current perception held by many, the U.S. deterrence posture of the Cold War was constantly evolving as the country tested and implemented ideas, keeping some and discarding others, and as non-nuclear capabilities advanced. In the more complex 21st century multi-polar environment, the U.S. is at the beginning of developing new strategies for deterrence and should expect those strategies to evolve as we get smarter about the threats it faces.

Regarding the second question, to be prepared to design and build new warheads, NNSA scientists and engineers must actually do it. Respecting the restructions of current legislation, the DSB is a strong supporter of exploratory and advanced development activities, which is the focus of the Stockpile Responsiveness Program at NNSA, with the provision that concepts can be carried through to prototyping and flight testing.

Mr. FRANKS. The December DSB report says: "The lead time for obtaining a modernized force is long and the U.S. is starting well behind Russia and China's efforts." We heard this same message yesterday at our hearing with General Selva and General Hyten.

Would you please explain why the U.S. is lagging behind Russia and China's modernization efforts and what could be done to shorten this timeline for the U.S. to catch up?

Dr. JOHN, Dr. ANASTASIO, and Dr. LAPLANTE. The U.S. is lagging because the Russian and Chinese started their modernization programs 20 years ago. There is little we can do to catch up, and delays in support for modernization will only increase the gap. Care should be taken in the current modernization efforts to ensure flexibility in the new systems (e.g., open software architectures) that would allow their rapid adaptation to changes in the threat once they are deployed. In the meantime, there must be investment in sustaining the force that is currently deployed for as long as possible and for engaging in a more comprehensive approach to deterrence as discussed in the answer to question #47. [Question #47 can be found on page 56.]

www.ingramcontent.com/pod-product-compliance
Lightning Source LLC
Chambersburg PA
CBHW080814280726
48660CB00018B/3433